GOLIATH

If you think that the only alternative to Spiro Agnew is violent revolution in the streets, David Harris has news for you.

This is a book of non-violent revolution, of peace, of love, of alternatives, of hope.

This book is a message from David Harris, from inside a federal prison. ("I don't feel like I'm leaving America so much as just getting in a little deeper.") It looks beyond the bounds of governmental politics toward a politics of life—and a possibility of a future in America for us all.

GOLIATH

DAVID HARRIS

AVON
PUBLISHERS OF
DISCUS • CAMELOT • BARD

AVON BOOKS
A division of
The Hearst Corporation
959 Eighth Avenue
New York, New York 10019

First Avon Printing, September, 1970

COVER PHOTO BY JIM MARSHALL

Printed in the U.S.A.

INTRODUCTION

It is dawn. The house is cold, and the sky is a glorious pink. My husband David is away in prison. Having been denied parole, he will be there for at least two years of his three-year sentence. I have just nursed our son, Gabriel, who is not yet old enough to make the trip to Arizona, where the prison camp is. David and I feel close and happy. Perhaps you will sense some of the joy in him as you read this book.

David thinks of this book as doing his work for him on the outside, as his opportunities for work on the inside are limited. David's work is to attempt to move the hearts and the minds, and thus the actions, of men and women away from fear and impotence and toward a position of upright humanity. He is a nonviolent revolutionary. He believes that together we can all regain our eyesight and see, not through the eyes of America, but through the windows of our own souls. For when a man sees clearly from his soul, he may be in a position to claim his life for himself for the first time since he was born. And only then, standing responsibility for his own actions, can he begin to build a new decent world for all men.

Goliath is the nation-state. Any nation-state. But for two reasons *Goliath* was written about America rather than any other of the 130-odd nation-states. First, David Harris was born and raised here. He is a home-grown, milk-fed, honor-roll, football-playing product of American culture. He has seen America as every other eagle scout has seen America, and he speaks American. Second, America, due to her superior technology, her great wealth, and her enormous power, is currently crushing lives more efficiently and in greater numbers than any other country on earth.

Concerning the title: David has fretted and fussed, thrown it away and taken it back again for want of another just as good. It is a perfect title, except that the author's name happens to be David, and some confusion as to the intent of the book can arise from that fact. There is only one chapter about David Harris versus the State. The book is really about you and me, and what we must do to keep from being crushed by Goliath, and then what we must build in place of it— something which has not yet been built in the whole history of mankind.

JOAN BAEZ HARRIS

January, 1970

CHAPTER 1

Out of Denver

The highway cuts into the meandering angle of the slope, snaking out of Denver toward the sky. To our left a stream flanks the road in thin sheets of ice. On the cliffside, the waterfalls have frozen into hanging draperies. Our exhale makes stiff clouds on the windows, and we must rub holes in our breath to see the road.

The storms that enforce winter brew at the peak of the giant backbone that runs north and south and divides east from west. Its white head pokes up like an American dowager queen with the open plains and meadows of Iowa and Indiana trailing behind her as the scattered edges of her winter train. The deities of winter hold court in Colorado. Our car makes its quick way up the throne, through the villages and settlements where the houses huddle together and give a solid front to the storms that roll off the mountains and batter the men against the mountainside. Across the gorge, clinging to the stream's thin rock border, the Rocky Mountain Express inches up the grade with four diesels and ninety-seven cars. When the Express blows its whistle, the sound freezes a solid note hanging over the stream for just a moment until it too is driven to find shelter and warmth and disappears.

We have been rising, through tunnels and over ridges, into mountain meadows clinging flat and untrammeled like outlaws in the steady thrust of the mountain. And up again, scaling the peaks on ropes of concrete laid by a thousand hands blue and cold even under the gloves and wrappings men wear into the mountains. The landscape is thick-white, studded with tips of buried trees drowned in winter. The land waits beneath the snow with only the little rock flowers to hold its banner. The rock flowers are blue and scarce.

We have driven and driven, and there is no more up left to drive. The mountain stops at the trailing edge of heaven. Up now is the belly of clouds. Up is the wind so cold it burns. Up is the sinking sun that bounces off the mountain's helmeted white head. Standing in the snow, I can feel my boots begin to leak.

Facing west and following the line of the gorge, we can see the bodies being loaded in the San Francisco harbor.

We can see the lives being stacked in Denver and packaged in Reno. The faces are being tied up in Albuquerque and burned in Los Angeles. The moans are being shipped from Des Moines on flatcars to be stored in Chicago. The children are being stamped and sealed in Baltimore, and their older brothers inspected in Atlanta. It is a clear day, and we can see for miles.

The mourners are being marched from Portland to Seattle for an exhibition, and Cheyenne hangs the widows in front of City Hall. The old men of Phoenix are crated and ready for burial, and in St. Louis mothers' breasts are being made into bullets. There is no room for the hungry in Minneapolis, so they've all been shipped to Florida for the winter. All the people without faces are being ground up in Detroit and fed to a steam press in Cleveland. In Pittsburgh the amputees have been given a ferris wheel.

In Memphis the rich use empty stomachs for napkins, and the poor are waiting to inherit the air force. In downtown Houston you can trade your son for a twelve-foot mounted smile and a plastic bucket. In Philadelphia the screams are being given rifles.

The sky has turned its cheek to the sun. Before night it is drawing its last full breaths of light which flush its face like the faces of children in the snow. In Trenton the vagrant souls are being burned on a platform in the Civic Center. The flames reach sixty feet to claw at the smothering belly of darkness.

CHAPTER 2

In the Beginning

In the beginning, there is man.

I am man. You are man. Man is us. Calling ourselves men is an admission of our incompleteness. Not that the idea of man is somehow a fragment or a lesser being. But for all our philosophy, we can attach no finality to that description. Our humanness is an approximate statement of location and direction. We do not know what humanhood is. We know only that we are there.

We are used to definitions. We are used to perceiving the being of things in their immediate presence and appearance. We live in a sphere crowded with objects. There are chairs and tables, desks, stoves, automobiles, lampposts, houses, and kitchen sinks. These things are definable with a word, or string of words, honed and fitted into neat circles and squares. But there are no words to encompass the mouth that speaks them.

To accomplish the exactness of definition requires distance at least. Definitions flow from separation, from the absence of common experience. We can define a chair because we are not chairs. If we admit that being men has all the form of a common experience larger than any one of us, definition becomes impossible. There is no perspective from which it can be done. The words we might use are included and subsumed in the experience itself. If we could define ourselves, that definition would have to stand as evidence of our lack of substance.

We might say that living is pain or work, or maybe an encounter between joy and insoluble deflating mystery. Human life might be something that is to be endured and exploited—or glorified. I suspect that with each or any of these statements we would not be describing man but rather our experience of him in ourselves and in our perception of the world. Such attempts are bound, by force of our condition, to be metaphors. To define ourselves, we must claim to be complete and all-inclusive. I, for one, can make no such claim.

Without definitions, we are left with only a location and a direction. We are left with our perception of our condition and of our possibility. We, man, are an unknown, and our lives become explorations. We have only what we do and might do. Unable to define, we are left with our experience—a form of knowing, not from the edges looking in but from the inside looking out. We can talk about the things we have seen inside and outside of ourselves. Such sights are what we seem to know, and in their whole collection they seem to be where we are.

In the beginning, we are men in America.

CHAPTER 3

Doing

We spend our lives doing things. Our encounter with the world is neither stable nor passive. Living seems both a process of change (we can all look backward and recognize our alteration in the motion of time) and of action (unlike rocks, none of us is self-contained and therefore must engage in an area beyond that of our bodies, if to do nothing other than gather sustenance). This is all *Doing*, and Doing is the source of our experience and hence our transitory home.

In the present, we often think of our Doing as a process of affecting other objects. The hand reaches out and moves the salt shaker, and this is Doing: the salt shaker has moved.

We picture our Doing: the cogs fall in place; the larger cogs move, the level falls, and a motion is imparted to the final spindle. We treat our Doing as a relationship between functional, defined objects, ourselves included.

A man does his work: he stoops and lifts, straining the muscles that run in the small of his back, and with a ripple of strength places a box on a pile. A man does his work: as the metal forms come in a slow procession past his post, he reaches out and places four wires in the second opening and solders them with a quick motion of his hand-held iron. We locate our Doing in what it is done to, not in who does it and how it is done. In such a way, our encounter with the world is made a series of services on, to, and for the objects that surround us. We are then separated from and controlled by our endeavor.

The process of Doing is our extension into the world around us. It is both an expression and a means of perception. Our hands are a good example: a hand fashions and makes signals, conveying the will and intention of the larger body. At the same time, a hand feels—it informs the larger body about the shape and texture of anything it encounters. It is both output and input, shaping and being shaped. The process of Doing is not generally as contained or as simple as the immediate relationship we have with our hands, but it is similar. It is often a complex progression of actions, feelings, positions, words, motions, and silences all strung in a bewildering and intricate dimensionality.

Even in its most complex forms, Doing is a two-way street. In expression, in the immediacy of an act, we establish our presence. From the position and with the form of that presence, we learn. We learn by perceiving. We perceive according to

14

where we are—according to where our expression has placed us and the tools it provides. We then act with those tools. If we look back from this ongoing process, we find we've changed. Our extension into the world has made us different. It has given us a past, a present, and a future.

Doing does not simply affect its object. Doing is a cycle strung between *doer* and *done to*. It is our experiencing. We are located in this dynamic. Doing shapes our experience, our experience shapes our selves, and our selves do.

In that sense, what we did is where we are, and what we do is where we will be. The present kindles the future. Our present shapes the agents and forces that will compose future presents. In an infinitely complex pattern and process, we have made ourselves and will continue to do so.

CHAPTER 4

Polis

We are much more than we seem.

We have each anchored ourselves in the notion of *I*. We try to see ourselves as separate and distinct from those around us. We identify ourselves with the unconnected singular. The plural confuses us; we generally understand it as an addition of singulars—a lot of singulars stuck together. We tend to see anything beyond the physical existence and seeming completeness of our bodies as a simple quantitative problem. One plus one equals two. *I* plus *I* equals *Us*. Such logic applies to pebbles but not to people. The addition of one man's vision to that of another is not simply two visions side by side. It is two visions occupying a common space. It makes one vision springing from two sources. Like transparencies laid atop each other, the nature of the vision has dimensions beyond either of its sources.

This plural existence is politics.

The word "politics" springs from the Greek *polis*. A translation of the phenomenon of *polis* would be roughly "the common life." The *polis* was actually a place in ancient city-states, an area generally located in the center of town, often including the baths. In this central place the Greeks hung out. It was a concrete representation of the sphere of common circumstance where individual lives synthesized into a larger whole. Unlike a physical place, the *polis* was not entered and then left behind as the gateway disappeared down the street and around the corner. It could not be left behind any more than the language that grew from such a *polis*—the set of terms, symbols, and attitudes commonly invoked—could be discarded on the way home from the central place. The *polis* is a larger circle that includes and surrounds smaller circles such as home and family. These smaller circles are not hollowed out of the larger but are included in the substance of it. The substance is that process of coming together—of shared being. The *polis* is a common mind and body (of varying form) for all of us it includes. It is the common context and mechanism for our experiencing.

The word politics has been emasculated over the course of history. We now take it to mean government and governmental function. Government was only one dimension of the Greek *polis*. The heart of the *polis* is its integration of any number of dimensions into a functioning whole. This integration is complete to its root consciousness in each of its participants. It is a common life. Treating *polis* as a common packaging of separate functions leads to fragmentation and wreckage. The common body then breaks from the common mind (in the familiar schizophrenic manner), and we are left as we are today— trapped with a singular identification and plural roles and conditions. We are left pretending we are alone in a room full of people.

Because of its basis in mutuality, the *polis* can also be seen as a state of being we attempt to reach. The resolution of a common life into a harmonious whole is true *polis*. We might say that we are presently in a false *polis*: totality without harmony, commonality devoid of sharing. We are elements in a common culture that is simply an enclosure. We are simply apples in the same bag. The commonality has become a state and lost its vitality as an inclusive and ongoing process. This might be variously described as insanity, oppression, totalitarianism, captivity, or fratricide.

Our doing is the substance of our politics. It too must be seen as a plural. It is not the doing of any one person we live within. This common doing, this sphere where lives overlap and blend, can be seen as our larger body and mind. After looking at it for a while, I see it take on patterns. These patterns of doing are expressed on a continuum that extends from solid and stable form as institutions (such as government and corporate capitalism) to transient and variable form as behavior (such as manipulation and theft). In looking at our larger existence, at the extent of our doing, we may understand a little more about what we do and what we might do.

In the idea of *polis*, the decision to live is a political one. The terms that decision is made in, their expression, and the forces they exercise are the elemental base of a common life. We each make that decision in the context of all of us. In the political dynamic, the decision for each of us is made by us all, and each of us makes a decision to and for each of the others. In that way the *polis* is born and grows, both beyond and inside of its participants. The life of the *polis* is the shape of our *doing*.

We are a very big sphere. The Greeks recognized only one sphere larger than the *polis*. That all-inclusive pattern was *deos*, the gods. I doubt my capacity to talk about *polis*, much less gods, so I will content myself with trying to picture the pursuance of the common life.

CHAPTER 5

Chicago

The city of Chicago is under siege. I have been here for three days, staying with Rupert in his apartment on the edge of Woodlawn, and we do nothing but scurry from shelter to shelter. The city of Chicago lives under a siege laid by itself. Like the penitent and the insane, Chicago uses the whip on its own back. The mind of Chicago is at war with its body, and Chicago reels, punching itself in the ribs and wheezing and bleeding with torn lips. This is my fourth trip to Chicago, and each time I try to visualize the city I am overwhelmed by the image of a titan in the middle of the continent, seized with devils and bellowing and pounding on its wounded body with fists.

Inside this behemoth, the ghastly has become the familiar. The state of war is taken for granted. The sky is so heavy with smoke that I think the city is burning. But if it is burning, it is a slow burn. I never see flames in Chicago, just smoke. The smoke bellows from a forest of stark and naked stacks with their open barrels trained skyward, vomiting a black drizzle that settles on the roofs and uncovered heads of the city. These siege cannon are grouped together in veins that roam across the face of Chicago. Interlaced with the forest of brick pillars is the huge steel suture of the elevated railway. Its rattles give the streets a constant hum, breaking any quiet that might filter through the city's roof. In the morning the trains disgorge troops for the continuation of the battle and in the evening return the troops for their nightly role, while the victims of the siege spend their day building.

Like a city under siege, there seem to be no exits from Chicago. The air is foul with the smell of rot, as though the dead had been tucked into niches and crannies unreachable by sight but continue to exercise their presence in the odor of the buildings and sidewalks. The grocery stores are stocked with aerosols and perfumes designed to disguise the air with flower petals and leaves from trees no one in Chicago has ever seen. But the smells hide in the cuffs and creases of clothes and in time seem to have coated the nostrils of the men in the shops and the women at their ironing boards, so that what seemed pungent to me was as unnoticeable to them as the odor of their own sweat. When my ears are devastated by noise, they seem deaf to the shouts and screeches, as we are all deaf to the beating of our hearts. These deaf-mutes, who must scream to be heard above the roar of the city's war upon itself, are Chicago.

The city is simply the larger soul they all reflect and worship. A man cannot run from Chicago, if Chicago is his eyes and nose and feet.

The siege is on Chicago like a flood. It is knee-deep on the street corners and laps over door-steps and seeps into even the smallest particles of space. There is no life outside the siege. It is every-where—the one bond, the universal cohesion—pounding all lives into a single pulp. There is much traffic on the streets but very little life. In the open areas of the city—the boulevards and parks and intersections—the people hug the edges and keep as close as possible to shelter and insulation. The siege keeps an ominous, brooding presence stretch-ing the city into a million taut and brittle patterns that cross and collide and wrap about each other, probing and moving and running, each concluding that the only sanctuary is in occupation.

News from the beleaguered city filters through the encircling army of screeches and hums, rattles and knocks. It climbs over the deadly range of the siege cannon. It is the sound of breaking glass, the sound of a man blowing full breath into a horn to place a single note beyond the reach of himself and the city. These sounds are the refu-gees wandering the streets: the sounds of men laughing, a solid and brassy thumping from the dim buildings, a scream rising on frail wings and circling the spot where the screamer sang into the billowing siege. The dispossessed wander about Chicago sleeping in the brick corners and frozen

22

sewers: the gentle touch hurled from a window in the righteous rage of those who wait, the soft sounds of lips chased from doorways by squads of babble, the thin straight lines of sight slashed and knotted by the occupying battalion of rage, the outstretched open hands lopped from arms leaving a city of bleeding stumps. Over it all comes the wail of official Chicago waging its war. The Crown Prince of Fear rushes back and forth across the city in blue and white chariots armed with flashing lights and sirens and numbered badges of dispensation announcing and enforcing the siege. The people back off the street as he passes in a blur of yellow light. "Long live the Prince," shouts the siren. "The siege is here. Everyone to his business. Long live the Prince's siege."

Yesterday, a dead man was found down the street from Rupert's apartment. A second grader found him. The man's face had been blown away by a shotgun. He was lying on the sidewalk a block from the schoolyard. His body was in a puddle of blood that had crusted brown and hard; on the front of his head there were small wet pools in what once had been eye sockets. We heard the scream of the official truck come to carry his body away. In a few minutes it receded into the awakening din of the city. The second grader went on to school.

On the same day, Sam and the one we call Willie the Mouse were leafleting the draft board building. The building is a large concrete square in the middle of the block. Across the street is a Catholic high school. During the lunch hour, the school's football team came over and beat Sam and Willie until they couldn't stand up. When they got out of the hospital's emergency room, the police came and warned them that if they came back they would be arrested for criminal nuisance.

That evening, there were eight people in the office when a wedge of squad cars and a paddy wagon broke out of the night and stopped. Sixteen policemen began to search the office. They threw the mimeograph on the floor and turned over tables and chairs. The drawers of the desks were emptied on the overturned bookcases, while two patrolmen frisked the staff. One man spent all his time stepping on a scattered pile of leaflets. When the office was wrecked, the sergeant in charge took a bag out of his pocket and threw it on the couch. "You're under arrest for illegal possession of narcotics," he said. Bail for each was set at a thousand dollars.

This morning, the nearby high school went out on strike. The students were outside shouting at the building and letting the air out of the tires of the cars parked along the curb fronting the blank brick face of the school. The old principal tried to shoo them away, running out the front door and waving his hands. The students laid a barrage of rocks on his head, and in ten minutes fourteen squad cars arrived. The police kept their distance from the kids until a brick caved in the

24

front window of one of their cars. The brick came out of a crowd, and the police ran after the fleeing students. When they would not stop, a patrolman drew his service revolver and put a hole through the leg of a thirteen-year-old. The bullet entered with a small puncture and made the front of his thigh look like jam.

An hour ago, the radio carried a report of the murder of a policeman. He was found in an alley with his throat slashed. He was twenty-seven years old and had been a policeman for a year and a half. "The Chicago police have begun a massive manhunt for the murderer. Anyone with information concerning the crime, call the twelfth precinct station."

Long live the siege, the Prince's siege.

CHAPTER 6

Flight

The plane claws its way out of O'Hare Airport. A snowstorm is rolling off the wide stretches of Iowa and Illinois and lapping at the edge of Chicago. It looks as if we'll be the last plane to make it out before the storm reaches the lake and closes the landing field. The airport's thin line of blue bulbs has been slowly snuffed by the tumbling bodies of fog. The plane seems to be impelled along its line of flight by a roar that seeps into the cabin as a cluster of tiny vibrations filling the seats and tray tables with a hum and then a murmur and sometimes a bounce. With each bounce, the wings dip a little, and suddenly I realize that I am riding in something that has no real bottom, no base on which to rest except its forward momentum.

A plane flies because it can rise faster than it can fall. A plane is a man making progress up a down escalator. A plane is not like a bird. A bird flies on top of the air, like a leaf on the surface of a pool. It catches the breezes and with the motion of its body transforms them into flight. A bird embodies an existing force; a plane creates and applies its own energy. A bird doesn't violate the air—it dances with a lacy partner composed of nothing more than nothing. A bird is buoyant. A plane is so heavy it flies: it can apply enough energy at a succession of points to trample the gravity that would bind all its separate ingredients to the ground. It is obvious that men built planes and God built birds. I would like to be a bird, but I feel much closer to being a plane.

One row closer to the first-class cabin and across the aisle are three men getting rapidly drunk. The first man, who was originally sitting alone enduring the plane's explosion out of O'Hare, must be fifty years old. He is wearing a loose-knit shirt and sportcoat. His face is red and beginning to break up at the edges. The energy that keeps the face glowing has grown narrow with age and cannot keep the lines off the corners of his eyes and no longer supports his cheeks, which have begun to sag and fold. His body widens as it gets closer to the chair's pivotal point. He looks more natural sitting than standing up. The two others joined him after the plane reached a smooth and steady stride upward to its cruising altitude. They are soldiers.

The first has dark hair and a moustache. On his chest are a number of small colored rectangles and brass medallions. His sleeves are rolled up over a pair of arms that look distinctly dangerous.

Each arm is covered with dark hair and swells back conically from a broad hand. After seeing his arm, I flexed mine and was able to run a ridge down the top of it from my elbow to my wrist, but it still looked flat. The first soldier is always clenching and unclenching his fists; his arms are everywhere, making broad descriptive motions in the air and flailing his drink around. Every now and then he turns to his buddy and grapples with him, punching him on the shoulder and coming as close to wrestling as he can in a set of three twenty-two-inch seats. The second soldier is taller than his friend and blond. Of the three, he is the observer. As the red man and the soldier with the arms wind into a bellowing conversation, he listens on the edge—laughing at the jokes, adding a word or two but intent on the drink in front of him on his tray. His two seatmates have become louder and louder. The first soldier does most of the talking. The red man laughs, his lips curl back, his set of yellowed teeth open, and he emits a rough and jeering sound. The first soldier is telling war stories. As he tells the stories, the red man bends forward in his seat, getting closer and closer to the storyteller. The soldier talks louder and louder.

"Me and Jimmie" (he motions to the blond soldier), "we was in Ben Ho for maybe a month. We was drinkin' every night. Not good shit like this" (he motions to the empty airplane bottle of whisky and knocks it off the tray), "but booze so bad it was like puttin' gasoline down yer throat.

'Bout the time we was really gettin' into Ben Ho they shipped us into the middle somewhere. Put us down in some little gook place. Can't remember the name. Just fulla gooks runnin' round making noise and lotsa dogs like us, and there's dust all over the place bein' blowed around by choppers, and everybody's runnin' around shoutin' things. Couldn't find no bars so we just found some shade. It was god-awful hot, so hot the flies couldn't stay in no one place for but a second, 'fore they burned their feet. We just found some shade and sat. I was just thinkin' how good a beer'd taste. Maybe even somma that Jap beer. You know, if I was willin' to drink Jap beer, we musta had a thirst." They all laughed.

The red-faced man begins to talk. "Yea, I know that Jap beer, it's like piss. So bad. . . ." But the soldier had only paused and restarts the story.

"Well we was in this village—wasn't really more than maybe twenty of them straw shacks but everybody called it a village, which was fine by me cause I couldn't say its name, I mean its name was like tryin' to wrap a string around your tongue. I'd try and I'd end up just spittin', so I called it the village like everyone else. Anyhow, we was in this village maybe two days when the sergeant— this big son-of-a-bitch from Tennessee—he tells us it's time to move. I thought 'bout that goddamn Jap beer till we was out in the jungle.

"For them first three days we never saw any gooks. I mean the lootenant he was always tellin'

29

us they was around, but all we ever saw was them damn mosquitoes. Them mosquitoes was so big they could stand flat-footed and fuck a turkey. I mean they was big. We was wadin' through swamps and lookin' over our shoulders and swattin' bugs, and there weren't nobody to be seen, 'cept one of them old farmers every now and then. On the second day we heard a big noise over near this road, and we bellied into the mud and started lookin' but nothin' happened, so we got up all wet and started walkin' again. Found out later that a mine had blowed the leg off a nigger sergeant in the second platoon. They said you could hear that nigger yell all the way back to Ben Ho. I believe it too. Them mines is fierce. Mean mother-fuckers. I mean mean. Them things don't give you no chance. Put yer foot down and it gits blowed to shreds."

His face clouded, and he drank again.

"Next mornin' we walked into another one of them villages. It musta had a name, but it weren't no easier than the first one. We lined 'em all up and looked at 'em, and the lootenant he'd shout at 'em and talk gibberish, and they didn't say nothin' 'cept maybe talk a little gibberish back at 'em. I went into one of them huts, and I tell you it smelled like a shithouse. I mean it stunk of fish and shit, and I was real glad when the lootenant he tells us to burn them huts. I figgered I was doin' them people a favor. The lootenant he sent a coupla gooks back in a chopper to be interrogated."

The word "interrogated" hangs in his mouth and has to be pushed out syllable by syllable.

" 'Bout noon we got outta that village, and then the shit hit the fan. We weren't but half a mile outside a it when they jumped us. I mean they jumped us."

The soldier stops and takes a long hit off his drink. He finishes it and swishes the ice cubes in a circular pattern, drains the last drops and puts it down. He turns back to the red-faced man who has been waiting, half bent into the soldier's seat.

"Me and Jimmie was over next to each other behind some palm trees and we started poppin' at em. Jimmie" (here he elbows his buddy), "he put a grenade in the middle of a whole patch of 'em. Shoulda seen 'em fly. But we didn't have no time to watch. I mean it was goin' fast. You get one of 'em in yer sights, and then you see four more. I finished two clips of bullets when we heard that chopper come in. Them things come in with their side doors open and big 50's lined up in the door blastin' the hell out of everything. It come in like a lawn mower on that jungle. There was leaves flyin' and trees blowed apart, and I stopped poppin' and watched it for jest a second. 'Bout then the lootenant hits me on the arm and sends me and Jimmie and a coupla others over to the left. 'We gottem on the run,' he says to me, 'git around there an' cut 'em off.'

"So we moved round behind some trees, lookin' over our shoulders all the time, and we come into a big open space, and at the other end we seed four of 'em in a cluster. I stopped and popped one of 'em and hit the ground, and the others scattered in the bushes and begin to pop back at us. I hit Jimmie and says, 'They gonna try to git the one out there in the middle. Nail 'em when they come out.' Sure enough one comes sneakin' out, and I let go at him, and he ditched back in the brush. Then he come out again and I got him in the leg, and he didn't come out no more. We popped 'em for a while more, and then they run off into the bush, so we moved across that open space. When we got across, that one gook was lyin' there in the middle. Jest movin' a little, sorta rockin' real slow from side to side. I'd blowed half his belly out and when I stood over him, he didn't even seem to see me. The others was lookin' off in the jungle for gooks, and Jimmie calls me to come on. So I just looked down and finished him off clean. I didn't look back but once, and when I did he weren't movin'. He's jest dead lyin' out between them trees. I felt sorta sorry for him, but then I started wishin' I'd got the other one too 'cause I heard Big Samuel had got it back on the road. When we was all together again, Big Samuel was just laid out all knotted up like he died in the middle of a twitch."

The story seems to have exhausted the first soldier. He sinks back in his seat for a moment.

The red-faced man is nodding his head and shaking it from side to side and looking wistfully at the storyteller. The two of them open the only alcohol left—a small bottle of dinner wine. As soon as it is poured, the soldier's heavy arm embraces it.

The plane is moving so smoothly that it is impossible to tell if it is moving at all. It is a movement in suspension. My ears have become accustomed to the whirr of the engines, and my eyes have accepted the limitations of this long floating cylinder. If I look out the window, we seem to be submerged in a sea of ink. There is so little light that depth can be perceived only as far as the flashing bulb on the wing tip. After that speck of red, there is only black, a black so thick that it comes forward as a solid surface as though this whole enterprise of flight was drawn on a slate. The only dimensions are in the plane itself. The space around it is dimensionless because it is impossible to conceive of such space. I have no way of knowing the implications of a position 37,000 feet above the surface of the planet. It is impossible to relate to that unknown and unknowable space, a sheer blackness that for any of my purposes is empty. The atmosphere the plane cuts through is so large it disappears.

Yet we plunge through it. As I look out the window I begin to feel it flowing past me. The cabin lights are out, and most of the passengers are sleeping. The glare and reflection have disappeared from the windowpane. Everything is black outside with a tiny red dot in the corner flashing. The darkness is tangible, I can imagine myself reaching out and grasping it, I can imagine myself shaking it as I would shake a sleeping man. I would shake the sun up to draw its silence from night's dormancy to the growth of day. I would dive into it and swim for the burning orb of the sun, stranded and sunken in its depths. It is night, bounded only by the arms of God. It is night, and I can only be a watcher. I can observe and describe and content myself to deal with the darkness my own eyes and arms embrace.

The two soldiers and the man with the red face have been joined by a fourth man. He has moved up and is sitting in front of me. He leans back on the seat as though it were a crutch for his body. He consumes all of the seat's space. His face enters his neck in waves of flesh that break against his shirt collar. In contrast to the first soldier, he never moves anything except his head, which swivels the least possible distance. He seems barely able to supply his huge body with the energy it needs to function. His lids rise only far enough to enable the minimum of seeing. His body is a wall—his lips form its only gate, and his words exit like refugees. His lips are an animation on a blank and unmoving surface of flesh. He is talking to the blond soldier. "You know," he

34

says, "I'm so fat I don't need an overcoat." Jimmie, the soldier, laughs without really smiling and looks straight at his drink.

I want to cry.

CHAPTER 7

A Dream

After the pilot announced our passage over the tip of Colorado, I shoved my feet as far forward as I could under the fat man's seat and fell asleep.

I dreamed in the infantile fascination in which we all dream. That fascination is not innocence, for dreams, like childhood, have nothing to do with the absence or presence of sin. When I dream I always feel as if I know things. In this way, dreaming does not seem as though the mind has broken from the process of previous knowing and gone blank, become once again a hollow sphere. My dreaming stands forward to me because it is a unique progression. The dream contains no experience of repetition—it is fresh at every moment. Inside a dream is a boundless present, uninfringed by the past and the soon future. An extension through space yet in a single tense. Thought without the partition of memory.

I dreamed of myself in a suffocating dark. Only my body has light. It is fluorescent, containing a glow within the boundaries of its flesh. The black-

ness opens into a room. There is a man at the other
end of the room. His face is covered with pancake
makeup. His eyes are lined with black grease-
paint. I walk to a point on the floor before him
where the angles of his pigeoned feet join. I can
see only his head and the gray wall behind him.
His right hand enters my vision. In it is an old
pistol, which he proceeds to cock and aim past
my head. He fires it, and his face disappears in
an explosion of gray smoke. The gray smoke becomes the head of another man likewise dressed
in a plaster face with sunken eyes. For a moment
he looks numbly around him, and then his hand
strikes his forehead with an open palm. Between
his fingers runs a thick black blood. The first
white face appears again and fires the pistol. Out
of the smoke another pancaked face emerges. It
is a lady with a bright orange plume tacked onto
her hat. Her hair is pinned up along the base of
the hat's rim.

In an instant, a trickle of black blood begins to
run from under a few loose curls. It grows until it
surges down the lines of her neck, and she ab-
sentmindedly plucks at it as if her hair had broken
and fallen out of its assigned place. The first face
appears and fires past me at a third victim who
grows from the smoke and reaches to his eye. Out
of the smoke rushes a surge of blood that clots
along his cheek. The first returns and fires his
fourth shot, and his own face appears in the smoke.
Slowly, blood begins to dribble from the corners

of his lips. His eyes grow wide with disbelief and confusion.

The stewardess woke me up just as the plane began its run over the long apron of water that laps at the end of the runway. Joanie is waiting at the landing ramp.

CHAPTER 8

Subject/Object

It is both traditional and convenient to see a society such as America as an object. We visualize it as buildings, offices, bureaus, and physical implements. In so doing, we locate society in its appearance. This leads us to ascribe political and social reality only to those elements of America that seem external—those institutions or services beyond the pale of any individual's hopes, terrors, impulses, dreams, and self-considerations. We grant truth to those things that have distance from us. Using such an analysis, we treat society as an entity separate from the people who compose it. The analysis makes out that America leads an objective existence—an imposed order growing out of forces and conditions distinct and separate from its participants. Society then is treated as an *other*, and we, enmeshed in its forms, are logically led to treat ourselves as objects in a larger play of static and finalized patterns.

I don't think America is an Object. In my experience, America has never resembled the straight and flat lines that such an analysis implies. It is more than a series of institutions, and it is governed by more than a simple mechanics. I won't deny that America contains objects and therefore a level of objective existence. But to ascribe the totality of its existence to those objects is like seeing only apples and no orchard. America, instead, can be considered a living entity that exists on a scale very difficult to visualize. It is an organism that exists beyond the perimeter of our physical form. Its scale gives it a quality unlike the quality we associate with our particular lives. It is a giant whose footsteps encompass everything we see. Our position is not outside or distant—we are within that footstep. We are occupants of its form. We know it by experiencing it. We live as its contributing elements.

The Mohave Indians believe that men have a "greater being." This being is an aura that extends beyond the limitations of the body. It is a force carried in the presence of a man that acts in the world without immediate physical visibility. It is a man's spirit roaming without the confines of a corporeal presence. Other men can be affected and even controlled by such a spirit. They in turn can use their medicine to impel their own greater being into action. Their image of the greater being leads the Mohave to consider the world, and their gathering in the world, in dimensions we rarely recognize. They assume that a man's doing enters his environment in the activities of his "greater being" so that the lives of people camped three days off are shaped by themselves, and vice versa. To many of us, this seems to be idle spiritualism. It may, however, be a quite adequate metaphor. We might say that each of us shapes the context for us all. We might say that America is the composite "greater being" of ourselves, the Americans.

To me, it makes sense to say that America is done. There are America and Americans (those who do the phenomenon of America). The society is a way of pursuing life, full of ritual and accepted processes.

A more inclusive explanation might be to say that society is a Subject. Far from a separate object, it is the largest extension in the orbit of the participants' selfhood. It is not necessarily a formal, conscious, or reflective process. The demons of the ancients were the externalization and symbolization of their experience and experiencing. They explained, formalized, and pursued their feelings and encounters as spiritual creatures. Moderns use society in a similar fashion. The forces framed within the social context are the means of being for those within it. These forces are then experienced, and people's assertions in response to that experience further shape that context. In this cycle. the society proceeds. America moves on as a way of being.

As an acting subject, society is our common extension. It is our larger self. It was, and is, men. It is what we know, and in turn it becomes our way of knowing. It should be no surprise to see our ignorance and delusion reflected in America and to see America bent on a task of stupefying those within it. If we, in response, treat our extension as an object, giving it its own existence apart from its source, we condemn ourselves to a choice between functional insanity and death. The mind leaves the body, the soul departs from the form, and we are left observing our hardened and finalized selves beyond our reach or control. Such separation makes us watchers of our dissection and disembodiment.

To exist, a society must be done. Its life is provided by the lives generating within it. In that sense, it is a participatory phenomenon.

We seem to have been enslaved in the process of carrying out the projection of our lives.

CHAPTER 9

Into Los Angeles

Julian and I got our first glimpse of Los Angeles when we peaked the Tehachapis and saw down the slope into the broad and flat plain that spreads out like water from the base of the mountains. Far across the alkaline flats, we saw a textured brown cloud.

The highway widens the closer we get to the city. As the barren, rocky slopes melt we begin to make our way through smatterings of civilization. A long string of faded pink houses extends and loops and corners iself into squares that advance along the badlands like a stucco posse. A tree has been planted in front of each house. Each tree is crutched with a redwood stake. At precise intervals in the progression of stakes, one to each tree and one tree to each house, there are driveways. The driveways hold themselves in mute asphalt attention as the newly paved road marches by. The road bends at the street lamps and suddenly ceases as it passes the last house and encounters open space without its cinder-block legions. The bibs of the houses are covered with new lawns. They grow in fragile tufts and have the appearance of a boy's first whiskers.

The lawns are protected with short wire fences. These fences and the house eaves are all hung with red, white, and plue plastic pennants. The colors seem to consume the sunlight that hits them. They just hang in limp, triangular shapes, without reflection or movement, like the poised teeth of the front porch. There are no pennants on one of the houses. The "NO DOWN PAYMENT, EASY TERMS" sign has been pulled out of the lawn, and a station wagon is parked in the driveway. The house has a dog, which sprawls under the parked car and moves occasionally to lift its leg on the seedling tree. Except for this one, all the houses are waiting; the streets are empty. Across the broad face of this settlement, someone has staked a line of bright red, white, and blue signs: "NOW OPEN. NORTH DESERT ESTATES. BUILT-IN KITCHENS. LANDSCAPED YARDS. COMPLETE REFRIGERATION. OPTIONAL SWIMMING POOLS. BUY NOW. NO DOWN PAYMENT. EASY TERMS. TIRED OF LIVING IN THE CITY? TRY SPACIOUS DESERT LIV-ING. EIGHT DIFFERENT MODELS. CREDIT. VETERANS' LOANS. RELAX IN THE SUN."

The highway swings in toward the pink houses before it straightens for its run into Los Angeles. The sleeping dog seems to have heard us and runs after the sound of our car through the empty streets and across the freshly seeded lawns. It clambers over porches and past the little trees. After dragging down a loose string of pennants in its path, it throws itself in a seizure of barking against the hurricane fence that cuts the houses off from the highway. We last saw it swaddled in plastic pennants and, spread-eagled, biting the fence.

Los Angeles was named "City of the Angels" by the Spanish after they had successfully crushed the Indians who used to pass through the area on their way to gather acorns and roots. The triumphant Spaniards saw it as a heavenly place, populated by unearthly messengers of God.

We never entered Los Angeles. It was just suddenly upon us, like an ambush or a vision. The sky thickened, turning from bleached blue to a shade of concrete. The highway widened to eight car widths, and we began to pass outcroppings of neon and plastic. Then rising out of the open space along the road comes a man's face in three-quarter profile. His eyes are downcast on the line formed by the buttons of his coat. He is dressed in a black suit. Behind him is a stew of greens and yellows with the occasional shape of a leaf protruding from the blended scene. His face encompasses an abiding sorrow that holds the whole visage intact from the square of his jaw to the roots of his graying hair. To his left is a quotation in big, black block letters: "MR. SCHWARTZ TOOK CARE OF EVERYTHING." Under that a line of smaller print reads: "Herbert Schwartz Mortuaries. Your friend in need." The face and its message rise out of the side of a hill. The rest of the rising mound is a deep green manicured lawn. In the center of the green, a string of gilded letters is propped up facing the road: "HERBERT SCHWARTZ MORTUARY."

On each side of the letters is a statue, cast in plaster and reaching after the style of Athens. Each sits in the middle of a fountain. The one on the left is a seated woman staring across the freeway toward a twirling orange neon spiral announcing "BEEFY BURGERS." Her torso is swathed in a flowing garment. Her neck, long and thick, and her head, topped with a curly bouffant hairdo, extend out of the top. Her mate in the fountain to the right has a cloth dropping from his shoulder to his loins where it wraps once and falls to the ground. His breast is bare and ripples around the heart. His short cropped hair is topped with a laurel wreath. The wreath is painted bright green. His hair is brown and his body a luminescent pink, swaddled in the blank plaster of his wrapping. The woman is pink too. Her toga is violet, and her rising mound of hair is yellow. Her lips are a deep ruby color. She is still staring at the hamburger sign as it lights and lights and lights again. A funeral is winding up the hillside, but it is too far from the highway for one to tell which of the figures is Herbert Schwartz. Julian

46

thinks he must be the man in the white toga at the front of the procession of dark suits.

The highway is built over the city on concrete pillars. From its heights you can see a distance crammed with avenues and pale-colored stucco buildings. Until the city's vapors ascend into an omniscient muddy cloud, the angels live level with the elevated road. Each angel seems to have its own prerogative powers. There is a twelve-foot-tall sweaty football player surrounded by lesser female angels with blue M's stitched to their chests. He looks straight at us and explains that because of the small blue tube in his right hand, no one can smell him even when he sweats. His neighbor, the cowboy angel, just sits on his horse and watches the sun go down in an orange explosion over a string of purple mountains. He is looking the other way and doesn't say much. He and his suspension in the sunset seem to be due to the ten-foot package of cigarettes he smokes. The one after him has a grease that he puts on his scalp. Before he puts the grease on he looks very much like Julian. He has a faint trace of pimples, and his eyes are downcast and lonely. After he puts the grease on, his hair becomes a slick package, his eyes bright, and on each side of him long-haired delicious women gaze in devouring glances. Julian runs his hand through his dry lump of curls.

The lovers gambol along a sunny beach that faces an ocean of transparent green. Each is trim and wrapped in an unending delight. All of this was possible because they deposited their paychecks in a bank on Fairfax Avenue next to a shoe store with boarded windows. Blotting out most of the schoolyard below, the angel of mercy asks you to give money to a child with bright cheeks and hollow eyes. The guardian angels are parading missiles behind a flag that is fourteen feet across, and the angels of justice are running a black man for mayor. The angel of judgment has just massacred bad breath with an unrumpled red tube, while the angel who brings success in all affairs is driving a Pontiac in her miniskirt. The angel of deliverance will fly you to New York so fast you can't digest the thick slice of roast pig she lays in your lap. If you don't like pig, she'll give you oysters if you just call ahead of time.

Just before we reached Santa Monica we turned off the freeway and descended into the city's less ethereal confines. The last thing we saw was an immense woman at least forty feet long, lying on her side. She sprawls on a tiger skin rug in a loose dress. The dress plunges at the neckline to reveal an expanse of flesh that rises in two protrusions capped with edges of fabric. Each of the breasts is a good six feet across. There isn't a flaw on their massive presence. "Yes," she says with moist edible lips, "you can buy me a Coke."

At the bottom of the off ramp, a girl in shorts is selling newspapers. Julian buys one. It tells us that Frank Sinatra has a new wife, the mayor is building another freeway, and the president just gave a medal to a kid who had his legs shot off. Overhead, the forty-foot woman can see all the way to the ocean, which seems to be paved over with auto exhaust.

CHAPTER 10

Julian

Over the evening traffic, the sun is slowly strangled into an orange globe. The dying sun stares like a single flaming eye as the gray runs off the freeways, rooftops, and storefronts to encircle it. Then it expires, leaving a legacy of an hour's light.

But the city seems to have waylaid the gentle sun for plunder. The day is dead, but its stores of illumination are in the hands of its assassin. Los Angeles proceeds to light itself. The wires are connected, the switches are thrown, and strings of fragile bulbs chase the black wake of might into the corners and across the yards. Down the avenue, a string of blue lights surrounds a shoe store, and a glittering market is capped by a flashing red arrow.

Julian left an hour ago. He passed the flashing arrow and melted into the lights. He left when he heard the police were on his trail again. As was usual with him, he left with a soliloquy. He rumpled his hair, veiled his eyes in mimicry of what he considered to be a tragic stance, and spoke, gazing into the avenue. "Well, David," he said, standing on the doorstep in a rumpled sports-coat, "I've got to split. They're on me again. Yapping at my heels, giving me no peace. I'm a hounded man, David. I think I'll go to Paris and show my manuscripts to Sartre." Then he left, past the market piled with cornflakes and beef stew in cans. Julian doesn't have any manuscripts and never did.

Julian wasn't born Julian. He was born Charles V. Lemon, son of wealthy fruit growers in the San Joaquin Valley. The house of his youth had three stories, all painted white, three cars in the garage, and a backyard of orange groves. It was five miles outside of Bing, a town with two banks and a packing shed. The former are owned by Basil Lemon, Julian's father, and the latter by Basil Lemon and Stanley Rathmore, who owns whatever parts of Bing the elder Lemon doesn't. Julian lived there, getting drunk on Fridays and Saturdays and flirting with Mexican girls, until he was eighteen and went on to Stanford University. His father sent him to Stanford to acquire the breeding and contacts necessary to carry on his name and position. After three years, Julian disappeared from Stanford and showed up at my house.

He came at four o'clock in the morning with a French girl. They had met at our rally in the park. He had been smoking dope all day and was ready to stick square pegs in round holes. She explained in broken English that she had been in America all summer, didn't like it, and was leaving in three days. Julian responded by taking her on a guided tour. He drove her to the mountains, discoursing throughout the journey on the existential character of American life. She was French, and he was sure she must know Sartre. When he reached a large clump of trees he stopped and said, "These are the mountains."

"Ah," she said, brightening as he slowed from his discourse to the announcement, "ze mountains." He beamed and began driving to the beach. Along the way, he continued his discourse, at times breaking into halting French. She couldn't understand his French. At the beach he stopped. "This is the beach," he said. She brightened again. "Ah," she said, "ze beach." Then he drove her to San Francisco and showed her the sights, which were all closed for the night. They stood in front of each of his favorite hangouts, and he explained in rapid English what happened in each one when it was open. She nodded a lot. They reached my house at four in the morning and fell asleep in the living room. Two weeks later, he announced to me that they were going to be married.

"She understands me," he said. At the time, Julian was calling himself Alexander Molokov. He sniffed some white powder out of a packet he kept in his perennial sportscoat and continued. He spoke with inspiration. "She's my mysterious lady. She's absolutely quiet, but she takes it all in. All of my encrusted soul and mad entangled life is in

52

her hands. She knows like a secret witch." He said all of that in one breath, never moving his face or lips. He talked with his hands and wrapped the words in a thick mumble. He then turned to her and ran his hand along her cheek. "N'est-ce pas?"

She had been intent on watching my goldfish, three of which were sleeping at the bottom of the tank and the fourth was floating belly up on the surface. With the touch of his hand, her eyes snapped to him and then to me. "Oui. Yes. We are going to be married." Then she smiled a big smile at the room in general. "You see, Harris. My god, what a woman. She understands. At last." He then went on to explain how they would settle in the area and start a discotheque called the Vincent Van Gogh Memorial Vision Factory. They would live in the back room, where Julian would write his novel and entertain his friends. Three weeks later Julian was drafted.

He and Sylvie, his bride to be, fled to Paris with the money he had made selling marijuana to defense workers in Sunnyvale. He presented himself to her father and announced their intention to marry. He was dressed in a dirty shirt and quoted William Burroughs to her father throughout his introductory speech. Her father promptly had him arrested and Sylvie committed to an asylum. Basil Lemon flew to Paris and bailed his son out, and Alexander Molokov, who had just changed his name to Julian Burroughs, became Private Charles Lemon, U.S.A.

During his basic training at Ford Ord, Julian receded into soldierdom. His hair was decimated and he had a shirt with "LEMON" in big letters over the pocket. For eight days he was squad commander until the sergeant found him reading *Naked Lunch* to his squad while they stood in formation. He was sent from Fort Ord to Hawaii for photography school. Once in Hawaii, he began to feel more like himself, whoever that was.

Julian rented an apartment in Honolulu and was soon established. In two weeks he was surrounded by a gang of Hawaiian cohorts. In the daytime he spliced film at the base, and in the evening he peddled dope and listened to music in his little house. It wasn't a bad life. He sat around at night making rapid philosophic pronouncements to his henchmen. He had even begun to forget he was in the army. Then he met the Mafia. Three of them arrived at his house one night and flattened his nose. They left with a warning, that if he peddled any more dope on their island, he was a dead man. The next day, Julian applied for a psychological discharge on the ground of extreme fear.

"If I don't leave this island, they'll kill me," he said.

"Who'll kill you?" the psychiatrist asked.

"The people who are after me."

"Who are they?"

Julian thought for a moment. "It's a long story," he said. "I don't know who they are. They just appear at night and beat me. I think they're Russian agents. I did some underground work for the Czechs when I was younger. Worked under the code name Molokov—Alexander Molokov. I must have secrets they want. Look at my bruises." With this, he pulled his shirt out and showed a purple splotch on his ribs. The psychiatrist was looking out the window at the palm tree and tapping his pencil on the desk.

Julian was given two weeks' leave to pull himself together. He took the first plane to San Francisco, burned his uniform, and hitchhiked to Salt Lake City. In Salt Lake he got a job as a night watchman in a concrete pipe factory. He rented a room in the Hotel Buford. After being there two months, he heard a knock on the door. He opened it and there silhouetted in the afternoon sun was Basil Lemon. He had two policemen with him. "Son." he said, "you've got to go back to the army."

"I'll give you a choice," Basil Lemon said, poking some of his extra flesh into his pants. "You can fly back with me or go with these gentlemen." He pointed to the policemen. One had a billy in his hand and the other's gun was drawn. The sun flashed off the barrel into Julian's eyes.

"Well Dad—" Julian looked around the room and saw there was no escaping. That afternoon Basil Lemon and his son flew to San Francisco. At the airport, Julian excused himself from his father and went to the bathroom. In two hours he was in Palo Alto, where he lived for six months with Bertha, his two-hundred-pound lover.

Julian was in fine shape, living with Bertha who fed and kept him, until he decided to go to the demonstration in Oakland. He was arrested driving the wrong way down a one-way street, and the police found his habitual pocketful of marijuana. He was taken to the station house and booked.

The desk sergeant looked up. In front of him was a disheveled-looking twenty-two-year-old in an old sportscoat. "What's your name?"

"Julian Burroughs."

"Where were you born?"

"Mexico City."

"Father's name and occupation?"

"William Burroughs, writer."

"Is he alive?"

"Yes."

"Where does he live?"

"I haven't seen him in years. I think he's shooting smack in Tangiers."

The sergeant looked up at Julian from his papers. Julian looked back without moving his face.

"Your mother?"

"Sadie Golmquist Burroughs. She died in 1949 in Mexico City."

"How'd she die?"

"My father was drunk and decided to shoot a wine glass off her head. He put a forty-five bullet in the middle of her face." Julian lowered his eyes in memory of his departed mother, lying on the floor with her face strewn over the rug. He let a tear run down his cheek.

56

The arresting officer was standing against the wall and pushed his hat back on his head. The desk sergeant reread the form and looked at Julian. He just sat with his arms on his desk and stared. Julian didn't move. Finally the policeman spoke. "You were born in Mexico City, huh?"

"Yes. I was premature. They planned to have me in Omaha."

They took Julian to a cell, where he promptly took off his clothes. We bailed him out the next day, and he hid in Bertha's cellar until we had left for Los Angeles.

And now Julian is on his way to Paris. He walked out and faded into the bulbs and shadows. I am sitting in Los Angeles thinking that Julian had to leave. There was no room for him here. I even hope Sartre likes his manuscripts.

The newsboys are out with the late edition. They are on the street corners shouting at cars. Blue Bonnet won the fourth race. The mayor has decided to build a new freeway, and the president gave a medal to a kid who had his legs shot off.

CHAPTER 11

Reality

One of the tools we use to locate ourselves is Reality.

Out of innumerable experiences, insights, and conditions, we isolate those comparative few we find to be *real*. Out of innumerable possible actions to reach an object, we choose the *realistic* one.

With our notion of Reality we construct a means of being.

Our lives are an effort at making *realities*. When we make something real, we concretize ourselves in the world around us. For example, America has made the *threat of international communism* a reality. For the Yaqui Indians, living in the same hemisphere, it is decidedly unreal. Their reality is bound up in the worship of the forest.

A society produces and distributes Reality. It provides common mechanisms and processes for making things *real*. Societies are distinctive according to how they *realize* the world around them. I am concerned with that *how*. It is what we live with and, in the end, is synonymous with the *how* of our daily living.

I call the process of making something real a *logic*.

America has a logic. When we want something, America is, among other things, the way we go about getting it. It is not so much *what* we want, as *how* we get it. The *what* seems to flow from the *how*.

The logic of America reflected around us is an instrumental one. Most simply, it is the logic of "if A, then B." The easiest way to picture it is to visualize a machine. If you engage cog A, then spindle B turns. In this logic, the actor and the realization of his action are separate. The action is not contained in the framework of the actor. He and his act are instigators of a process which is beyond their control or involvement. For example: soldiers make war in the pursuit of peace; businessmen make profits under the rationale of common democracy. In each of these examples men act, but the intention of the act is in no way carried in the act itself. The actor and the act are a force designed to activate a distant process which supposedly produces the intended reality.

A man's act is an instrument in a process located beyond his existence. He is an input. A's leading to B is never left up to A. Since the act in itself does not lead to the desired result (A, in itself, is not B) this logic presupposes an overriding, qualitatively different entity which will actually make A into B. When activated in a society, such a logic necessitates the paternal and authoritarian state to make the needed translations. The state must be responsible for making acts of war into peace and capitalism into democracy, for they obviously are incapable of such changes in themselves. The first result of this process is the dispossession of a man from his actions. His actions are a function of the process that will supposedly *realize* them.

In this instrumental logic, the man who acts does not have a direct relationship to the things he wishes to come from his action. If he wishes B, he must instead do A. If he wishes peace, he must first do war. His actions have a direct relationship to an overseeing intermediary. He feeds the state, which in turn is supposed to satisfy his intention. His action then is an extension of the state. Reality ceases to be a function of those who compose it. Reality becomes a product of the state.

Looking for a moment at ourselves, we can see our intentions, our actions, and their results. Following the instrumental American logic, the three exist in complete disconnection. The act realizes neither the intention nor the supposed end. The act realizes the mechanism it is being done for and with. Instead of making our realities, the established reality of the state begins to make us in its image. We no longer carry out our intentions but make our actions a tool of the state in hopes it will realize them. In letting A take the place of the B we want, we become supplicants. We are the recipients of reality rather than its source. We become strangers in a strange land.

Whether or not this instrumental process leads eventually from A to B may be a secondary or an irrelevant consideration. (Although evidence seems to witness that it does not, five thousand years of war being the most obvious example.) What is primary is that despite rationalization and ideology, we experience and are shaped by the immediacy of A, not the promised resultant B— it is A we must live with. Whatever else comes of the process, those of us involved in it have been made powerless. In it, we are stripped of our rightful construction of reality. We are *unreal.* Our presence is that of dependence and servitude, not freedom and creation. Our doing ceases to spring from ourselves, and our lives become merely instruments in a process that grants us reality only as tools of things we neither create nor find ourselves reflected in.

In this logic, which leaves the actual fact of reality to a Great Other that we faithfully serve in return for morsels that help hide our pain, we cease to exist. We become an impotent pause.

CHAPTER 12

Existence

The most striking feature of this logic is that those practicing it must assume a vicarious relationship to themselves and their situation. When our doing is not an immediate process of making ourselves real (when the object and the intention of an act are not done in the act itself), a direct relationship to ourselves is impossible. To assume such a relationship, we would have to be present in the America around us. But in this logic, the only means we have for establishing our presence—our creation of reality—is denied us. We must then live in a situation we compose, but which is not of our making. We try to locate ourselves, but we don't exist. Overwhelmed by our need for Existence, we find someone else to be.

We use the word "identity" to describe the process of our presence in the world. If we can look out and find recognition of our Existence, we have an identity. To be without an identity is to be unable to perceive ourselves in the eyes of others. Without an identity, we are unreal. Identity is our concrete existence in the world. It is our reality.

Inside of the world, each of us is pursuing a relationship with himself. Forgetting the present we live in, we can imagine or hope for a situation where the growing self of that dynamic simply overflows into the world around us, with little trauma and discontinuity—like the first motions of a child. We can imagine ourselves making our own terms. But, resuming the present, American logic makes that an impossibility. For America has no available space for such growth. All of the surrounding culture in which we must make that indigenous expression is built on a logic that denies expression in its own terms. Such a presence in the world is its own source of being; it demands an immediate and conjugal relationship with reality. It is precisely this demand that the culture is not geared to meet and, consequently, will not allow. The state is the established source of being. Identity can only be phrased in its terms. Reality is America's. And America, beyond our reach, belongs only to itself.

So to exist at all in the implementation of this logic, we must be America. We must be as the state is because the state is synonymous with being. The "we" inside of ourselves, with all its potential immediacy and power, has nowhere to go. Making ourselves real is impossible within the state, so we must let the state make us real. We find something amid what exists, and we exist in it. This process is commonly called *"identification."* To achieve the assurance of existence in the practice of America is only possible through identification with the state. The more our participation in this American logic crushes us, the more we are forced out of sheer necessity to identify. The state holds out a collection of idols, behaviors, occupations, and successes, and from those we must choose our lives. The process of being in America is not unlike marching the starving into supermarkets at gunpoint.

In this condition, we each have four basic alternatives: (1) to follow the required process of self-nullification and assume the identity the state provides; (2) to construct our own logic in conflict with the state and run the risks of isolation and, if our isolated energies are insufficient, to maintain a separate reality—nonexistence; (3) to bond together in common groups and create smaller, more palatable, yet accepted realities within the state; or (4) to combine in pursuit of our reality and attempt to break the state's control of Existence. In this last alternative, we engage in the political process of denying reality to the America we know only as our negation.

The vicarious Existence implicit in doing America simply means that we spend our lives being something we never intended to be. Our constant engagement is in being someone else. When reality is carried on through an intermediary, our condition in the world is not available to us—it cannot be seen or shaped—for we are not available to ourselves. We exist as an *other*.

That Existence is America's characteristic. It is a formation of power. Despite its titular position as a democracy, America is not democratic. Its own logic prevents it. The tool defines the task, and its instrumentality is anathema to democracy. For democracy is more than a procedure of voting and more than common consent and obedience. The great appeal of the democratic ideal is in its demand for a common reality based on the dignity, validity, and power of its members. It defies the authoritarian state precisely because such a state denies its participants an Existence on their own terms. This notion of democracy is the hope of men for an indigenous reality. But a reality indigenous to its participants is precisely what America is not.

In America, reality is not exercised by the people. True, its members elect some of those who will in effect control them, but that is not an exercise of reality. In the context of the American logic, such voting procedures take on all the aspects of ritualized subservience. When our lives are formations of the state, we exist in a condition of unreality. The state is real, not us. This impotence is reflected in all that the state realizes, be it in governance, economy, or the small items of living from day to day. In all of them we are receptors of reality and not its source. In all of them, America holds the actual human exercise of power beyond our grasp. In all of them, we are never of our own making.

CHAPTER 13

Myths

One of the ways we can understand a system of politics is as a model of consciousness. America is a means by which we experience the world. It is a commonly occupied mind, a set of terms projected on experience, a lens through which the world is seen. Being a participant in America is sharecropping a cosmology.

The logic I previously described is the introduction to that consciousness. It seems to be the American taproot. Given that, we are living in an enforced reality. What remains is understanding the content and consequences of that world view.

Perhaps we can best approach it in terms of myth. A myth is a standard, archetypal pattern of consciousness. It is an interpretive means. A myth is a shaping of the mind. Myths are our tools for grappling with existence and our models for shaping it into realities. For example, the instrumental logic I have been describing is a myth. It is an aspect of our consciousness which determines our reality. The myth essentially says, "Without

America, you're nothing" or "If it wasn't for America, you'd be nobody" or "You can't buck city hall" or "You can't have everything, be realistic." Each of these, and many more like them, carry the implicit message that the American state is the source of reality. The myth may be carried in a story in which the hero reaches success through his diligent pursuance of that which exists. In it, the message is plain. If you want to be real, then you have to go to the things that possess reality, and America has it.

Such a myth establishes the impotence of the people and the omnipotence of the state. It is society's notion of the locus of the power necessary to realize things. This conception of power is the means for accruing energy to America's participants. Power is a function of the state. Those doing America then experience the world through this notion, act upon it, and embody it in ongoing institutions and behavior. The myth provides a framework imposed on the world in which we shape and locate ourselves.

Historically, we can see myths that make the function of myth clearer. One such series of myths surrounds the subject of trees. The Zulu in southern Africa consider certain trees to be the earthly form of spirits. For countless generations this myth has been venerated. To chop a tree needlessly was a crime punishable by death, according to tribal law. Such harsh penalties were invoked because of the way in which trees were perceived. This perception is a social function. America, on the other hand, perceives trees as a simple form of plant life, fed by water gathered in their root systems. Our tree myth makes cutting trees acceptable and, in many circles, a source of profit. What is important is that the conception of trees carried in the ongoing social dynamic shapes the experience, lives, and visions of all who participate in it. The myth involved is one of the tools society makes available for dealing with the problem of existence. For the Zulu, the spiritual and divine nature of trees is a reality. For Americans, the reality of a tree is generally found in the uses it is put to by those who cut it down. If we consider trees to be spiritual creatures, the world takes on a very different format. And we in response may develop a radically different form of existence.

America operates around a set of myths. They are all interconnected and overlap in organic relationship to each other. Taken together, they are an enclosed system of consciousness. Each of them is an interpretation of an aspect of the world. They all have concrete manifestations as the accepted form of man's venture in the world. They are the substance of the state. These myths are the organs of the beast we know as America. A description of them all is more than I can do, but I will try a few that seem to draw the outlines of a pattern.

CHAPTER 14

The Myth
of Power

The logic of America takes shape as a world of objects. Objects can only be arranged. They are recipients of action and gain meaning according to whom or what they are controlled by. Objects are without an indigenous existence. In the world of objects, Power takes on a very specific nature. Power is manipulation and coercion. Power is exercised *over* things.

We should keep in mind the dimensionality of a society. Power is not applied from a source to a flat surface beneath it. A society is composed of any number of levels of existence, and reality must filter from one to the next and so on. Power is passed on; its procession through society is implicitly participatory.

When the substance of Power is manipulation, the object of Power is control. Something or someone is powerful according to their subjugation of their environment. Within this myth of Power, the play of Power in the society is always oppressive, for the capacity to oppress is the manifestation of Power. Oppression, by definition, is the natural expression of Power. As this myth of Power takes form throughout the society, it offers two choices of function to an individual within it: having power over or being under the power of someone —oppressor and oppressed. It is important that we recognize that these two are not necessarily two distinct groups of people. They may be dual roles played by a single person or group.

The role of the oppressed within this myth is universal. Being oppressed is being a recipient of power's exercise, having power used over oneself. In that sense, being oppressed is a statement of our presence within America. Since the state is the ultimate source of reality, even those we consider the most powerful are always subject to it. A social elite exists as a function of the state. (There is a great difference between controlling and being a function of something.) The elite has a particular and important role in the state: serving as its priests, embodying its virtues, and performing its public rituals.

Being an elite may simply be a statement of proximity to the state's mentality. Its existence teaches a visible lesson of power, which the entire society must incorporate for the society to function. But it is an elite within a mass movement; though it may be psychotic, it is nevertheless a mass. Members of the social elite are more like trademarks than oligarchs.

Being oppressed is also the role in which the myth of Power is seeded and passed on. Having power exercised over oneself, one experiences it. This experience of oppression impresses the face of the state's power upon us. Manipulation also trains the people on whom it is used to its uses. It is the society educating its participants and extending itself.

The role of oppressor is that of intermediary for the state. The oppressors are the state's messengers, the couplings in the chain of Power as it makes its way through the layers of society. As they are subject to the Power applied over them, they subject those who fall in the order beneath their station. In this chain of Power, it is both possible and common to be jointly oppressor and oppressed. (Even the lowest echelons in America determine the condition of peoples around the world.) The two roles are descriptions of the flow of Power in the capillary action of society. Both are roles inherent in the conduction of Power through the American body politic.

The struggle of oppressed against oppressors is the conflict inherent in the myth. Men want to be closer to what they consider to be the source of reality. Within America's myth of Power, this struggle in the social milieu is the reordering of positions in the passage of Power. Those whose Power is strained and taxed by those before them

72

will seek a place of less encumbrance and more reward. This struggle is not necessarily against oppression. The oppressed may rise in various forms against the oppressors while still reinforcing the myth of Power, which is inherently oppressive.

Within this acceptance, the myth ensures a constant state of antithesis. This clash prevents the development of any commonality other than that which is found in the environment of the state. When Power is manipulation, the adherence and synthesis of the various elements of society to each other is impossible. Harmonious merger is unreal because each is placed in a position of contradiction to the other. The Power all engage in using or attempting to use precludes sharing and grouping for any purpose other than advantage. A society in which reality is accrued through manipulation finds its logical existence in stratified antagonism.

This conflict also takes place among the individual social participants. Oppressor and oppressed are contradictions. Yet existence in America is the concurrent practice of both. By definition, the myth of Power includes a conflict between aspects of the individual and collective self which is commonly diagnosed as schizophrenia by psychiatrists. In the play of Power, we are strung between its use by and against us. The individual participant is caught in a cycle of self-destruction, setting one's left hand against one's right. (In the politics of this myth, sanity is simply the quantitative range of conflict in which the person is still functional for the purposes of the state.) In the social practice of manipulation, the attempt to be real is a struggle against ourselves.

Oppressor and oppressed are indigenous to this myth. Oppression is a whole process. Its elimination is the elimination of the process and the myth in which it is born. Because the realities in the exercise of Power are contained in the quality of Power itself, change within the acceptance of this myth is a realignment and not a reformation. When Power is manipulation, it is only capable of the arrangement of objects. Its presence in the body politic ensures that the participants will be objects and that they will be controlled as such. The seeds of oppression are within the power itself. Hence, America's natural state is an ascending and descending order of slaves.

CHAPTER 15

The Myth
of Property

The world is a collection of resources which offer the malleable substance out of which we shape our physical existence. They can be used to maintain and extend ourselves in everything from the simple satisfaction of our hunger to the complex provisions of our farthest journeys into space. They form the mass of a potential reality. How they are used is an outcome of our perception of them. From that perception flows a relationship in which they are shaped and arranged. The practice of power as manipulation has an obvious result: America creates the myth of Property.

Property is an overlay on the potential of the world. In it, resources are arranged according to who controls them. Control is accomplished in the enforcement of the idea of ownership. In operation, ownership shapes the world's potential. Instead of resources being the meeting of needs, ownership is an extension of control. Thus when a plot of land is considered property, it is so not according to who needs it or might use it, but according to who owns it.

Property concretizes the vicarious reality characteristic of America. It prevents us from assuming a direct relationship to our most inherent condition: the existence of a set of physical needs we are all subject to. These needs are far from the heart of Property. Instead of pursuing them, Property dictates that we pursue ownership. The pursuit of need follows a logic of use. When you need something, you use it. Instead of using things, America demands they be controlled. In the dynamic of Property, ownership, not need, provides the right of use. The person who owns something does not necessarily use it. Ownership is the control of its usage. By controlling the use of resources, we control the people who need to use them. In fact, the person who owns a resource owns the lives of all who must use it. Need itself becomes simply another resource to be controlled in the exercise of power.

If the world were shaped according to our need of it, then its resources would be available as a function of that need: the hungry would eat, the homeless would build homes. Instead, resources are allotted according to the logic of power: the hungry are fed when it is convenient; the homeless are occasionally housed. But never are the resources available to them directly. They must live in the vagaries of ownership's philanthropy.

76

If their needs are met, they are met in the accepted context of control—based upon the needy's incumbent prostration.

Property transforms what is potentially a universal means of support into a particular means of control. That transformation occurs at the expense of our reality. The state is made the intermediary between men and their survival. Even the pangs of our hunger are unreal unless owned, and their satisfaction impossible without title. Property makes suffering a marketable product.

Need is something all men have in common simply as a fact of their physical existence. Property reflects none of the commonality inherent in the universal phenomenon of need. Need is all-inclusive. Ownership is fundamentally exclusive. It is impossible to shape the world and not in turn shape ourselves. Property etches the face of man. It prevents us from experiencing the world as a mutual exercise. The common house of need becomes the battleground of ownership.

As a social framework, Property is a mechanism for the location of ourselves and others. It is a means of gaining identity and the sensation of existence. In that process, ownership becomes our presence in the world, and men are according to what they own. Leading lives of ownership is a very specific reality. It is existence by exclusion. We are something by virtue of the fact that what we are is unavailable to anyone else: *we are be-*

cause others are not. The world that might be mutual affirmation is mutual denial.

This arrangement of the world is a pattern of existence. Property proceeds as our acting assumption that all of us cannot exist. In order to exist, someone else must not. Competition is the behavior in which this denial is exercised: all men take on the form of a potential negation to each other and are treated as such. Competition is based upon each man's isolation and each man's greed. The unanimous acceptance of this assumption makes it an enforced social condition. If we accept America, we accept Property. If we accept Property, we accept competition. Accepting competition, the only available behavior is isolation and greed.

In America, competition is the context for the contact of lives. It makes mutual destruction the common, accepted, and valued behavior between men. Suffering is its legitimate and natural expression.

Property is a negation of the common conglomerate man. The reality of a common existence of men as a harmonious whole is impossible within the acceptance of property. If all of us have an equal right to exist, Property obviously does not.

CHAPTER 16

The Myth
of Enemy

Enemy is the means for experiencing each other that is built into America. Since the world and the reality inherent in its uses are not commonly available, contradiction between men is a social given. Man is located in the process of mutual denial. Each person, then, exists as a threat to the other. This knowing according to the criterion of threat I call Enemy. Enemy presumes, seeks out, and does contradiction.

The American reality is located in antagonisms. To be real in the terms of the state is a process in which we are contradictions to each other. Our attempts to be real are then attempts to know our enemies. If reality's expression is contradiction, we are unreal if we have no enemies. If reality is located in negation, we must negate and be negated in order to be real. Enemy is the identity made available to each by the other and by each to himself. If enemies are what we look for, enemies are what we find.

It seems that the process of America can understand man only according to his division into enemies and allies to aid against enemies. America comprehends by choosing sides. Men locate themselves and are located according to their positions on sides of an antagonism that is generic to the state. We then do this to each other. When Enemy is the means by which we know each other and is carried on in our doing, it sees, pursues, and realizes only itself. Enemy is only capable of finding and nurturing enemies. It, like America, makes the world in its image and likeness.

Doing Enemy is a projection of existence. It denies that man might be a common experience. Of all the facets of man that might be made real, it realizes only those that divide and separate. Enemy fragments, not for the purposes of clarity and resolution but in pursuit of itself. Enemy can only be realized through the continual extension of separation. Separated, we have no experience which we share. In such disconnection we can only know each other as different and beyond the substance of each of our particular realities. We can see each other only as negations. In our eyes, the others have none of us and we none of them. Unlike our relationship to ourselves, we take them at face value. Their face, seen with the eyes of Enemy, is contradiction.

The only resolution to that difference available

within Enemy is destruction. Enemy establishes a contradiction between man. Doing Enemy is a question of eliminating the other pole of the contradiction—again and again as each new contradiction comes to view. Enemy severs any possible common process in which resolution might materialize. The other is always experienced as an opposite, a foreign and dangerous presence. We experience him as static and defined. A static, defined, and separate contradiction can only be nullified and destroyed. The acceptance of Enemy as our means of understanding each other is inherently an acceptance of a concurrent process of destruction. As long as Enemy is practiced, those around us will be *them,* and as we do Enemy we will be their destroyers.

In the world of Enemy, the other is *them.* In doing Enemy, we do *them. Them,* a collection of men devoid of an existence in common and possessed only of an existence in contradiction, can only cease to be in a bond of shared experience, which the use of Enemy denies. The use of Enemy fulfills itself in a world composed of us and others —a legacy of blood and of shattered and starving faces.

CHAPTER 17

The Myth
of Weapon

If, as Enemy presumes, the surrounding ex
can only be negated, then the force that is a
must be the pursuance of negation. Weapon
negation in full form. Weapons are a nec
one pursues an existance of enemies.

Weapon is the mentality of the state come to a
point. It is a particular shape. It is shaped to de-
stroy. Weapon extends a reality through the negation of contradictions. It enforces its reality. Its
use denies any reality inherent in that to which it
is applied. Weapon subsumes everything it encounters to the politics it extends.

Doing Weapon, we assume that reality is a function of control. Realities are not born, they are
enforced. Thus reality is the right of those whose
negation is the strongest. The strength of a negation is a function of mass. As a force, weapon must
overwhelm.

Other forces have other strengths. For example,

the strength of a seed is not in mass. The strength it uses to push a sprout out of the earth into the air is a result of its synthesis with other forces, even that of the earth it breaks through. It has strength through its creation of mutual reality. It brings all of the forces it encounters into the reality of its growth. Were it dependent on mass, a seed would be impotent; it is tiny. But a seed is powerful far beyond its size because it does not need to overwhelm in order to realize. It realizes by transforming the force it encounters.

Making a reality through the enforced nonexistence of everything outside of oneself means accruing enough mass to crush the *other*. It means becoming large enough to deny the resources other realities need in order to exist. Imagine bricking over a field, and you have an idea of the use of Weapon.

Mass is an effective force because it can apply a large quantity of energy in a single direction. If you throw a brick, most of its energy follows the direction you give it. Its effectiveness is dependent on its being nonvolatile. Compared to a brick, loose mud is volatile; if thrown, it spreads out in a number of directions. There is nothing in the mud to bind it in any direction that you might try to give it. If you tried to throw a handful of air, you would find it virtually impossible. In itself, a handful of air has none of the potential cohesion necessary for following a single direction. Its components, jillions of molecules, are pursuing directions according to what they are instead of what you want them to do. Volatile substances (in society as well as in chemistry) are ineffective if you attempt to use them as an application of order to effectively apply a force base fect of mass, as in the use of Weap reduce the number of directions to this, you must reduce the sources of rea since each source of reality will pursu indigenous direction. This means that t zation of Weapon is done to negate not it is used against but also those who participa it. For Weapon to work, it must have effective mass; for Weapon to work, we must all become functions of it. We must be reduced to an extension of another reality. That reality is the reality of the state. Weapon demands that we be subsumed under the social organism rather than being realized in it. Weapon is inherently authoritarian. Extended to its full form, weapon means that we all pursue nonexistence—both the butchers and the butchered.

The process of Weapon confirms the state it extends. It assures our immobility and the state's action. It assures the state's freedom and our slavery. The use of Weapon concretizes reality beyond our reach. With it, we can never make ourselves. It ensures the prevalence of the state. It feeds the beast America.

CHAPTER 18

Fear

Being in the middle of America, I am afraid. I think we all are. Our fear is a natural fear. America can only be experienced fearfully. Constantly subject to a reality which we receive rather than mold, we dangle over the edge of nothing. Our existence is out of our control. We are in the grasp of the giant America. We are in a flux we have no way of grasping; the power we have is dependent upon our acceptance of impotence; our existence depends upon our willingness not to exist. Such a life is frightening.

This fear is that of the mother whose child plays in the street, of the man working who may not work tomorrow, of the wealthy in the offices whose wealth may disappear in the fractions of a stock report, of the lover whose love may die in whimsy—the fear of those who can see themselves as nothing save what they are.

It is the fear of the trucker running his rig without a spare, of the family whose house is mortgaged past the attic windows, of the gamblers before a race, of the farmer standing in a soggy field watching another storm approach—the fear of those whom the world seems only to diminish.

It is the fear of Blind Jake who begs at the corner and of Mrs. Hobbs who just covered her furniture with plastic. It is the fear of the Chinaman who runs the hot-link stand and must walk six blocks at midnight with his day's receipts. It is the fear of Mrs. Plumber who owns four houses, and the rent from all four is always late. Of old John Diggs who is afraid because his son is gone away to the army. It is the fear of those who have no one and nothing to count on.

It is the fear of the minister passing the collection plate and of the men who work in the helicopter factory down by the Bay. It is the fear of Elly Diggs whose boyfriend left her pregnant and went to Texas. It is the fear of the patients in the hospital who sit all day and watch the plastic tubes drain and replenish their bodies. It is the fear of those who must live in the hands of others.

It is the fear of Oliver who owns and keeps a loaded revolver under the cash register and of Officer Kane standing on the corner watching everyone who walks past. It is the fear of politicians in an election and of the men who own the banks. It is the fear of those who sit on top and look down, waiting for the eruption.

It is the fear of the flock of neighborhood children who wander the streets throwing rocks at the dogs and of mothers who laboriously count their change before leaving the store. It is the fear of Bill Boit whose car is being repossessed. It is the fear of those who must stand at the bottom and look up, waiting for the collapse.

It is the fear of those who stand dumbly in the lines of the draft board building, waiting for the buses. It is the fear of the drivers who steer the buses through the traffic, sitting majestically over the view of the automobiles and lesser vehicles. It is the fear of the woman I read about in the newspaper this morning; she died after putting one too many needles in her arm. It is the fear of those who have nothing else to do and no one else to be.

It is the fear of men running stop signs, catching planes, and punching clocks. It is the fear of the work whistle and the jet plane. It is the fear that both the hungry and the gluttonous share. The fear of those who have no time to wait and see.

It is the fear of those who don't look in the mirror in the morning and don't ask questions. It is the fear of those who only have as many problems as they have solutions and as many steps as they have guarantees. It is the fear of those who only take cash and buy a pack of cigarettes at a time. It is the fear that tomorrow is always bad news.

It is the fear of tightrope walkers and albinos, naked men and Marilyn Monroe. It is the fear of the leaders and of those who do not follow. It is the fear of those who live behind big windows and last year's dresses. It is the fear of a nation of billboards—the fear of those who are watched.

It is the fear of Jesse James and of the old ⸱ at the nursing home. It is the fear of debt⸱ tired generals, and convicts doing ninet⸱ years. It is the fear of those who have wo⸱ of those who expect to lose. It is the fear of c⸱ sacrificial martyrs, and drowning men. It i⸱ fear of those who are waiting to die.

It is the fear of cripples, wage earners, mac⸱ operators, and railroad firemen. It is the fea⸱ the jailors and of the jailed. It is the fear of A⸱ of Jesus Christ, and of all the world's executio⸱ It is the fear of those whose future will be not⸱ but more of their present.

It is the fear of fat men, nymphomaniacs, house- wives, and ascetics. It is the fear of the boys on the corner putting the make on each passing skirt. It is the fear of the drunkards who live at Henry's Grill and of the diplomats who have never heard of Henry or his grill. It is the fear of barren women, unweaned children, and the rich. It is the fear of those who will never quite be satisfied.

It is the fear of slave traders, judges, soldiers, school principals, politicians, and those who own things they have never even seen. It is the fear of landlords, welfare workers, and the president of United States Steel. It is the fear that does not wish to be seen and likewise cannot see. It is the fear of those whose livelihood has become the buying and selling of the lives around them.

It is the fear of all of us—the lonely, the insulated, the harassed, the lost, and the blind, who only have recourse to fantasy; of the ones with illnesses no doctor can explain and feelings we can't quite describe; of the ones with speech but no words, work but no tools, family but no friends, houses but no homes. As with birds in a cage, it is the fear that comes from living without access to any of the things that make living real.

It is the fear that makes our titles blaze in neon and polished brass, locks our doors, arms our soldiers, and sets us aside to glorify and pursue our emasculation. It is the fear that makes the eye see only as far as the hand can reach. It is the fear that etches danger on the face of the land and steadies the grim resentment that has become our pride. It is the fear that reaps bushels of screams in the night and fills the day with lips tight in silence.

CHAPTER 19

Dispossession

Society is a composition of lives. It has existence as a setting for the care and nurture of men. It is rightfully neither our cradle nor our prison—it is our home. A society should not provide bondage but tools with which fetters are broken. If men have a world, then that world should be their affirmation. Looking about us, we find that men have no world at all.

If there is a crime we might ascribe to ourselves, America, it is the dispossession of mankind. From the agony of our forefathers we have inherited a condition that is our own denial. Rather than a steppingstone, we have been given a resting place. Rather than a preface to our liberation, the world we have shaped is the description of our servitude. In such a prison, our work is simply the extension of our bondage and our prayers an acceptance of our plight. Our rightful inheritance is life. Instead, our coffers are bulging with the infinite miracles of fast and slow death.

CHAPTER 20

The West End

The morning sun creeps along the edges of the sleeping houses. Back from the curb, it sidles against the doorsteps and windowsills. It enters its own absence and rouses the form of day with a slow sure touch on her back and legs. Before it is clear that time will pursue itself and the dogs will soon bark and the sun will rise to a broiling height, the morning is intimate.

Last night, I drove into Fresno from Los Angeles. Today, I will drive on through an enclave of fertile earth known as the West End. I have to stand trial in San Francisco in two days.

The sun's thin fingers roll back the dark blanket hiding the city. They play on the grass, sparkling it with streamers of light, and enter my mother's house through the kitchen window. Day pries at the lids of my eyes. Even as my body is in the kitchen making coffee and burning toast, my mind hides in the covers of my boyhood bed, demanding one more relapse into the release of dream before trying its unsure grip on the day. The day is free to blossom out of sleep, but I must travel before the heat comes down in long waves on the valley and blisters the roads. The day is free to save her darkness until it has died a natural death in the basements and undersurfaces, while I must snap to the call of hours that are not yet upon the bushes.

I am on my way to trial, where the government's attorney will open his leather brief case and pull out a filing folder stuffed with papers. He will admit it into evidence as Government Exhibit A. It is the government's record of the defendant. With it, he will show that at the age of eighteen I registered with the Selective Service System, that at the age of twenty I refused to remain registered, and that at the age of twenty-one I refused to obey an order to report for induction into the army. He will use it to prove that prisoner number 41844, myself, has no right to enjoy the liberties of walking the streets of America. He will stand behind his plastic-rimmed glasses and contend that the stuffed file he holds in his hand contains all of the issues germane to the court. The file is covered with smudges and handprints. It has my name on the front followed by a long number. When the government's attorney introduces it, he will hold it level with his shoulder for everyone to see, and everyone will look at it. There is nothing special about it. It's just plain brown and dirty.

The avenue winds out through the city past the Moonlight drive-in and the old Chinese graveyard where the weeds hide the gravestones. As it passes the stables, the avenue becomes a highway. There are no more rows of houses save an occasional stuccoed dwelling with a cow and a chicken roost behind it.

The San Joaquin Valley is the innards of California. It is the bed of what once was an inland sea. Fresno sits at its crossroads, like a blotted stain on a clean sheet of agriculture. The last edges of the city dribble into orchards and planted fields. The Sierra Nevada mountains form the east wall of the valley. The valley extends north to the Stockton harbor and joins the Valley of the Sacramento. To the south, the valley flows a hundred miles long and flat until the floor breaks against the Tehachapi Mountains below Bakersfield. I am heading west toward the Coast Range. At the outskirts of Fresno, everyone who can owns a tractor. In the middle of the city, there are people who've never seen a tractor except at a county fair.

The West End is its earth. Life is close to the ground. There are no big buildings and very few little ones. The men of the West End live by taming the ground and marshaling its richness into truckloads of sugar beets, melons, and grapes. The West End is also hot. It is not yet six-thirty, but already I can feel the heat accumulating in the air. By midday, the sun will fall full force on all of this flatness and drive thoughts of heat from the mind. To rise is to be closer to the sun, and it is hot enough on the ground.

The West End exists on a single plane. The heat, like a great weight, presses men against the earth. Afternoon, the temperature will reach 105 degrees. On both sides of the road the fields stretch until all the lines I use to order sight have narrowed to a point called the horizon. Even this horizon is just an empty space above the diminished and coagulated rows of plants. An occasional house breaks the landscape. In the city, the earth has been pinioned and subdued by these structures. Along Fresno's streets the earth is imprisoned with manacles fashioned of its own offspring. The trees it fed for so long have been coupled with its rocks and mixtures of its dark loam and strapped upon it, so that the earth lives on as caged patches of green and a quiet home for the dead. But here, in the West End, the arrangements of wood and plaster are less than the land. They are foreign objects that shock the eye. Here in the West End, the land is first. It is not yet broken; it is only indentured.

The flat buzz of an airplane hangs in the air. It has double wings and tanks strapped to its belly. The plane rises on its wing, swoops upon the rows of beets, and drops a blanket of poisonous fog. The fog settles on the leaves and on the ground and searches for whatever it has the strength to kill. The plane rises again over the power lines and descends on the field of string beans. On the other side of the highway, the night's wetness is lifting off the field. A light mist of evaporating dew

94

is over the ground. Before it rises ten feet, it has been heated to pure vapor and disappears.

The road has big cracks and ruts baked into it. Irrigation ditches run on either side of its disintegrating edges. Their banks are covered with long grass and cattails. Road signs encroach on the road's narrow shoulder. Some have half toppled into the ditches. Most are hand lettered: "PEACHES by the LUG" with a crooked arrow pointing down the dirt road. The more formal make a rusted and bullet-riddled attempt to advertise Coca-Cola or Burma Shave:

> Chickens in the henhouse
> Roosters like to crow
> If men laid eggs
> The Chickens would have to go.
> Burma Shave.

The signs lead like droppings up to the old wooden roadside stores. The stores are standard—not as a functional design as much as a result of the sheer fact of endurance, which seems to level all things on the valley floor. They have sagging screen doors, a chair on the porch, and a single gas pump in front of the entrance. They are far enough from the city that only the missionaries from Coca-Cola seem to have reached them. Even Coca-Cola hasn't been there recently. The painted advertisements on the building side have cracked and blistered. The girl holding the sweaty and dewy bottle of cold goodness has a peeling set of pigtails and freckles that have rusted around the nail holes. The presence of the stores is terse. They are passed quickly and only present themselves in one or two short words: "EAT" or "FOOD" or "EATS AND FOOD" at the larger of them.

Judging from the roadside, the West End is hard on machines. Along the two lanes of the highway between Mendota and Fresno there are a good two dozen rusting hulks. All seem just to have stopped, to move no more, as though the pressure of the big hot sky had pinned them to their places like a collector's box of butterflies. By now the scavengers have taken their wheels and seats. A few doors are missing, but otherwise they are whole corpses, outposts of the diminishing reality of 1953 when all the cars were squat with a pinched nose like a tied sack of bread, or 1941 when the cars had long probing snouts, resembling a turned-over fat canoe with wheels on it. The one youngster of the wrecks, a 1958 Buick, seems to have died under the strain of an insufferable load of chrome. In the West End, movement is never free of an obvious and everpresent inertia. The old men say it's the heat that does it. The young men say that the heat and the old men do it together.

An old bus is driving in front of me. It is full of laborers for the fields. They are packed along its rattles in rows of three and stare idly out the window. They are being hauled up from the labor

camp at Buell Crossing. After crossing the SP
tracks, the bus turns off the highway and onto a
dirt road. The road hides it with dust. Beyond it,
I can see lines of pickers stooped in front of the
morning glare.

The men can't hear the engine of the bus over
all the rattles. Riding every morning in the rows
of seats behind the driver, the men slowly learn
to trace the noise. There is a squeak that begins
by the front wheel and works its way backward
along the frame and culminates in the vibration
of the emergency exit door. There is another in the
roof that begins in the patchy ceiling and circles
the girth of the old bus's body like a cinch strap.
The seats are all loose on their moorings and assume a circular wobble as the speed of the truck
encounters the immobility of the crumbling road.
Outside, the edge of the road passes in flurries of
fox grass. Every now and then an irrigation ditch
crosses the road, and their is the bump of plank
bridges. As the truck turns onto the unpaved ranch
road, the men can see the pickers making their
way through the early red edge of the sun. The
pickers had started before it was light, when the
men were boarding the bus. Already the storage
bins have twelve trailers of melons to be packed.
The pickers have been working hard, trying to beat
the sun so that they might sweat a little less today.
The old bus, with "A.J. Samos, Labor Contractor"
printed along the peeling length of its body, de-

posits the men in front of the packing shed and is parked behind the kitchen.

As the bus drew closer to the ranch, the men were nervous and silent, trying to make their bodies accept the eventuality of work. Now they silently laugh at an unmentioned joke. The crew boss, Grady, with his yellow teeth and folding flabby cheeks, comes to tell them to stop sitting and get on the job. The men crush their cigarettes and enter the shed. The shed has a long angling tin roof and open sides. Some of the men wear cotton gloves to protect their hands from the rough hide of the melons. Others just tape the ends of their fingers.

The melons roll down into bins after being sorted and graded by the old men further in the depths of the plant. The first motion is to reach up with the left hand and grab an empty box that rides by on a conveyor. The bottom of the box is folded and placed on a small platform that rests at the middle of a standing man's thighs. Then the right hand reaches into the bin for a melon and flips it to the left which puts it in the box. The left hand arranges the melons in a pattern, fitting the proper number in each layer. Some melons won't fit right and have to be flipped back into the bin. A separation paper of flat cardboard is put between the layers of fruit, and another pattern is arranged on top of it. Then the top is folded and stamped with the packer's identifying number, the platform is lifted, and the box slides onto a belt which carries it to the sealing machine. If he is good, the packer will finish one hundred boxes before the crew boss calls out "cinqo" to announce each hour's five-minute break.

Before the sun beats its way to noon, the big boss has arrived. He drives past the gate and into the work yard in a white Lincoln convertible. His name is Patapolus, a short and swarthy Greek in pressed slacks and an open-collared short-sleeve shirt. He prides himself in the physical trim that hides the corners of his forty years, and through their sweat the packers can see him lift an occasional box. He acts busy and talks and watches and shouts until the half hour lunch break. It is too hot to eat inside, so the men lounge in the shade of the melon trailers and eat sandwiches. In the middle of digestion, the afternoon's work begins. By one o'clock, the men can feel their labor. The tall ones feel it in the small of their backs and along the hamstrings, which have been stretched and bent in reaching down to the boxes. The short ones feel it in their hands, which must spread to grasp the wet fruit as it arrives from the graders. The big boss and the straw boss walk the row of packers and watch each one, commenting to themselves and shouting at the packers. "Too bulgy," Grady shouts. "Too goddamn bulgy. Pack it right." He pulls the packed box off the conveyor and dumps it in the bin. "Pack it right or you won't pack at all." The men don't talk much when they take their five-minute break. They smoke and try to ease their bodies.

The men are given half an hour for dinner. They walk, dragging their feet through the dust to the cook's shack. They talk in low voices and occasionally laugh as they pass the back of the kitchen where the cook's helper dumps an armload of dishes into a pot of dark greasy water and then returns through the swinging door with the same armload of dishes, now dripping wet patterns on his apron. After dinner the lights are turned on in the shed. The pickers are out of the fields, but they have left thirty trailers of melons to be packed, and the day isn't over until all the melons are in boxes. The yard is dark except for the patches where the packing light seeps under the eaves and spreads like spilt milk along the dust. After dinner the big boss takes his car and goes, and Grady is left to bellow by himself. After ten, the last box is packed. The men wait in front of the shed for the bus to take them to the camp down the road. They must work again the next day, and each wishes to capture as much of the short night as possible.

An argument has broken out between Ramon and the young Indian kid. The anger of their voices carries above the agony of the bus trying to start. By the time the old bus has kicked over, they have begun to fight. The other men only look up. Ramon has the Indian kid on his back and is beating his face with his hands. The kid's head starts up, then Ramon hits him and his head bounces back onto the dirt and up again into the fist. The kid has a long gash on his face from Ramon's high school ring. When the bus approaches, they are shocked by the glare of its headlights, and the fight dies. Ramon sits in the back of the bus and the Indian kid in the front. As the headlights break over the road, Ramon listens, as they all do, to the rattles. He sees the billboards and the road and the bus and his skinned knuckles and thinks about the boss and the boss's big car. Some day, he thinks, he will kill the boss and Grady too. Not because he hates them, but because, past his hatred, he can conceive of nothing else that fits their position.

Near Los Banos, an hour's drive from where I last saw the bus, there is an old gas station and junkyard. Ten acres of rusting wrecks behind a rotting wood fence surround the pumps. A big sign on the fence reads "IKE'S GAS AND WRECKING." While I waited for my tank to fill and Ike rubbed an old rag over the car's windows, a plain-colored Dodge with a state seal on the door stopped in the gravel on the station side of the pump. It had a whip antenna and a screen of wire mesh that divided the front seat from the back. The two men in the back seat were dressed in khakis and the two in the front in suits. When one of the front-seat men opened the back door, I could see that the two men in khakis were chained together. The man who opened the door was middle sized with a girth beginning to break away from his belt. The second was maybe five-foot eight and Mexican with his hair slicked over his ears. The officer who seemed to be in charge walked the Mexican over to the restroom. As he pulled the smaller prisoner, the chains brought the other along in tow. The second officer walked behind the procession. He unlocked the handcuffs and stood outside the door with his blue-suited partner. As I was paying Ike for the gas, there was a shout from the restroom. The Mexican had jumped from the side window of the lavatory and over the wall into the junkyard. The second officer chased him and we could see them scrambling over the tops of the cars. The escaping prisoner plunged through the rusted roof of an old Nash and got stuck. As he tried to wriggle his way out the policeman fired a shot over his head and he stopped. He ran his hand through his hair. When the second officer and the Mexican reached the station, the Mexican was manacled with a pair of handcuffs run through the back belt loop of his pants. They chained him to the other prisoner with another pair, and then the officer in charge hit him across the face. When the escape started, Ike was standing behind them with the shotgun he had pulled out of the station. The Mexican had a bloody splotch over his eye.

As the car left, heading west, I could see the Mexican through the rear window. He was crumpled over in the seat with only the top of his head showing. The second officer was red in the face and still winded from the short chase. They passed a house with chenille bedspreads on the line in front. An old woman was sitting on the porch to sell the spreads to passing tourists. Beyond the "BEDSPREADS $2.00" sign, they entered the string of billboards. The tall prisoner just watched the gaudy signs that told him what he couldn't buy and would never be able to use.

I paid Ike and left. The heat had begun. It rose off the road in patterns. As I passed the bedspreads, I saw one with a big embroidered peacock. It had an eye in each of its tail feathers and watched the road with all of them. The old woman was smoking and watching the peacock. I could see past her to the mountains creeping out of the valley and toward San Francisco. Behind me the West End was a collection of green rectangles and golden squares arrayed in fences and dying roads.

I am on my way to trial, where the judge will spend most of his time nodding his head and making notations in a big leatherbound book.

CHAPTER 21

Country Church

Over the grade, the highway turns north and pursues an inland line parallel to the course of the coast. It passes the onion fields in Gilroy and the wineries in San Martin. The towns are clusters of buildings, growing back from the highway. Between the towns are strings of small fields and an occasional roadside church. In the fields I can see a few men digging and hoeing. On the right, two men are working on a ditch. One is standing on its edge, and the other is in it knee-deep with a shovel.

Along the line of their shoulders the dust has collected, and then, bursting from under the dust, lines of sweat have patterned their dirty backs. The patterns have become as intricate as layers of dust and the continued weeping of their bodies have met to make the men themselves ritualized hieroglyphs of their work. They have been working in the ditch all day. Beginning at the turn in Johnson's fence, they have progressed through the sandy soil to a point where they meet an imaginary line drawn from the last tree in the line of cotton-woods backing the distant house. Now it is time to stop work and bathe and eat. Billy Royal runs back down the road to get the truck. He guns the battered pickup through the bumps and comes to a stop in a spurt of road that clouds around the back wheels. The tools are dumped in the bed, and the men abandon their half-completed ditch for the sustenance of home and dinner.

After dinner the plates are hurriedly washed and the family is tucked noisy and scrambling into the corners of the truck, as the old headlights find their way to the church. The church shows its age in its cracked and faded front. Over the doorway are two signs. The first is stationary and old, like the rest of the building. It announces "Christ's Church of New Hope" to friend and stranger alike as they pass on the oiled road that stabs toward the hills off the highway. The other sign is a canvas banner strung between the protruding roof beams. It says "Revival Tonight" in fire-engine red with a small painting of an angel in the lower right corner. The angel is all blues and yellows. In front of the church, the yard is full of trucks and old station wagons.

Inside, the men and their women and children are sitting in straight-back chairs. Against the far wall is another banner. It says "Brother Gabriel Will Save You" in two-foot capitals, and in one-foot capitals "Believe in Your Sheperd Jesus." The entire wall is lighted with foot lamps, and the pulpit sits in the middle of the wall. On the left are Brother Gabriel's singers, four blacks in silver robes backed with an electric guitar, beating tambourines and singing. The singing is slow at first, and then the men begin to rock in their chairs and the women to clap. The singers begin to beat the sounds of their voices together, making a single, gelatinous, egg-shaped sound.

> Better get ready for the judgment
> Better get ready for the judgment
> Better get ready for the judgment morning
> My Lord is comin' down.

Some in the crowd have begun to shake. All their voices have joined in now. All except the children, who must watch and absorb, knowing little of spiritual ventures such as the one Brother Gabriel conducts.

In the first row, an old man with scrubby clumps of gray hair begins to cry. He hunches forward in his chair, tipping the rear legs into the air, and then leaps to his feet crying, "Jesus is our salvation, brothers. It is Jesus." There are mumblings and utterings around the room now, rising to the top of the music and then falling off and under its constant progression. Outside, the fields are asleep, and with the moon you can see up into the range of hills. Brother Gabriel enters through the front doors and comes down the aisle shouting, "Jesus is your savior, good people. We must find Jesus." He

106

claps his hands and moves slowly. "Tell us, Brother Gabriel, tell us about Jesus," the people shout. The audience is all denim and coarse dresses, and their shoes are beating on the floor. When Brother Gabriel reaches the platform, the singing dies to a low hum and then ceases. All of the eyes, those dry and those rolling in tears, are on the man in the black robe. To his left, off the platform, Sister Eustace stands in her silver robe. She has long pale blond hair that falls over her shoulders.

"Brothers and sisters, praise the Lord."

"Praise the Lord," the crowd shouts. The terrified children are quickly shushed and sit quietly in their pools of infantile fright.

"Brothers and sisters, I come here tonight to tell you that you can be saved. You can be redeemed. The Lord on high has sent his son, and that son is our salvation. You who have sinned, you who have ignored the Lord, who have chosen the path of the devil, you whose arms have shriveled and whose backs have bent, you who have toiled for the devil and forsaken the love of God, all of you can be saved.

"No one is too big or too small for Jesus. As he is the child of God, so all of you are his children. And with the mighty hand of his mercy, he shall make you whole. He shall give you the light. He will teach you to love him above all things and to fall on your knees and praise the day you heard his name. He is all and everything. Without him we are lost, and with his grace every day we are new men."

Brother Gabriel gestures widely and stops with his arm extended to the right toward the corner and the flag.

An old woman stands and shouts. She wears a blue smock and a shawl wrapped about her shoulders. "Yes brother, tell us more. Tell us how to find our savior."

"He is in your hearts, brothers and sisters. If you open your heart and stand up for Jesus, you will find him as I found him. You will see him walking through the proud fields of our nation toward you with his arms open to embrace you. Let me tell you my story, brothers and sisters."

Brother Gabriel pauses, and the room assumes the silence of expectation.

"Yes, I was a wretch," he shouts. "I was a sinner and a drunkard. I was a lost man and in the middle of my misery. As I was in the company of drug addicts, prostitutes, and filth, as I was rolling about in my sin and wretchedness, Jesus came to me. He came to me with a message as I was in the gutter. For I knew my plight. I knew I was lost, and in my desperation I asked the Lord for help, and he sent me his son. He sent his only son to my filthy life and said, 'You, get up, you must spread my word.' Yes, that's what he said, 'You, get up, you must spread my word. And I sprang to my feet, and since that day I have shunned sin and have thought only of Jesus. Thought only of our precious

Lord and his work. I have spread his word and will spread his word more. That has taken me many places, and everywhere evil is holding the upper hand. But have no fear, Jesus is our protector. . . ."

Brother Gabriel speaks for an hour. During the hour, the denimed people spring to their feet and praise good Brother Gabriel and good Sister Eustace for having come to them and given them hope. A young woman, no older than twenty-four, stands on the platform and confesses, asking for guidance. She is on her knees, with tears spreading along her cheeks. Brother Gabriel touches her, prays over her, and tells her to get to her feet and go forth. And she goes forth, with fresh cheeks and drooping eyelids. The plates are passed three times, and each time everyone gives until they can give no more. Sister Eustace in her silver robe passes the plates. With each donation she chides the giver to praise the Lord. "Bless you, Sister," they say.

The singers begin again:

> Better get ready for the judgment
> Better get ready for the judgment
> Better get ready for the judgment mornin'
> My Lord is comin' down.

The people file out of the doors slowly. Brother Gabriel stands at the door with a few words for each as they leave. An old woman has to be helped to her truck by her son. Billy Royal's shirt back is covered with sweat. Brother Gabriel has been sweating too. Beads of dripping salt run in the angles of his face and soak the collar of his robe.

The next day, Brother Gabriel's bus drives along the oily road toward the highway. A large tent meeting is scheduled for the evening in Dos Palos. The sides of the bus stand out in bold letters: "BROTHER GABRIEL, Messenger of God and Christ"; and in smaller letters, "with Sister Eustace, God's own angel"; and in still smaller letter, "The New Revelation Singers"; and under it all, in letters the size given to Brother Gabriel, "BRINGING YOU THE MESSAGE OF OUR SAVIOR, JESUS CHRIST."

Next to the lettering is a painting of Jesus that runs up and down the entire side. He is in a robe with a staff in his hand, and surrounding him in waves is a halo of red and blue light. Around the red and blue is a field of gold. Under the blood dripping from his lacerated feet is an inscription reading, "He shall save us all." The agony of his body, which is dripping blood from a series of wounds, doesn't seem to have reached his face, which is calm unto blankness.

The bus passes the field where Billy Royal and Jess are continuing the ditch. They only see it after it has passed and is making the turn onto the highway.

I am on my way to be tried in a room with no windows. The doors will be closed, and through their tiny slits you will be able to see out into the hall, which also has no windows. The hall and the court will be lit with fluorescent tubes. The light is perpetually empty and glazed. It is absorbed by the imitation wood paneling in the court. The judge will come out of a door in the front of the courtroom, and everyone will rise. Those who don't will be thrown out by the bailiff.

The further north I follow the highway, the more the open space is encroached upon. In its place are the steel arches of power poles and the lines of housing tracts. Monster earthmovers roar to and fro, shoving the rises into flats and gouging the flats into houses and roads.

CHAPTER 22

Trucker

The last time I was on this road, my car broke down. It was night, and the neon lit the dark like small fires posted along the highway. The lights swam the road in packs with night seeping into each of the partitions in their glare. I stood by the road for two hours looking for a ride. When I found one, it was with a trucker I saw coming out of a bar. The bar was a squat building pushed back off the road. Its parking lot was full of semi rigs and trailers. The trucker, who called himself Ralph, was on the arm of a woman with huge red lips. Her face was pasted so that it looked thick, and her walk was an unsteady rhythm from side to side. She was pushing up against his side in a blouse cut down to the end of her breasts and pedal pushers strung like a tight wire across her hips. When they reached the edge of the highway, she clawed at Ralph's neck, and he laughed. She retreated to the bar talking over her shoulder. "You look me up on your next run, you hear Ralph?" Ralph just laughed again and then exploded his laugh with a belch. After the belch, he laughed twice as loud.

"Got a ride?" I said, walking up the road edge.

Ralph looked up and focused. "Make it," he said, pointing to his rig, and I hopped into the cab.

We moved up the highway through his twelve gears. Ralph was steering with one hand and gulping coffee and pills with the other. He offered me both, the first out of a thermos and the second out of a plastic bag. "Only way to make these night runs," he said from behind the coffee.

We cruised along in silence for an hour. Outside of San Jose, Ralph raced another rig. The two of them were side by side on the empty highway. Ralph finally lost. "It's this fucking load," he said. "He must be hauling air. With the same load I'd beat his ass off the highway." His face assumed scowling lines around the mouth. He was young, and the scowl made him look like bitter fruit picked early from the vine.

Ralph stopped at a big turnout where the highway bends along the San Francisco Bay. There were three other rigs parked. He got out and checked his load. He went to each cable and tightened it with an iron bar. Near the far exit from the turnout, there was a sedan parked with its lights off. The other rigs seemed to be sleeping. Ralph got back in. He pointed to the car. "Faggots," he said. "They hang out here looking for truckers. Watch this."

113

He blinked his lights. The car answered by blinking its brake lights. Ralph blinked his again, and the car backed up to where it was only thirty yards in front of us. Ralph was talking through his teeth. "Fucking queers," he spat out. "Just hang out here looking for truckers. They get a gang and jump you when you're trying to sleep."

A thin man got out of the car and leaned against it. He lit a cigarette and looked at Ralph's truck. He couldn't make out what or who was inside the cab. He could see him intermittently when the lights of passing cars splashed onto the turnout. He was nervous and snuffed his cigarette, only to light another. Ralph began talking in a whisper. "If he comes over here I'm goin' to give him this." He reached under the truck's dash and pulled out a claw hammer. "Right between the eyes, split him in half."

The faggot just looked at the truck. Ralph tried to coax him on in his whisper. "Come on over, queer. Just come over here and I'll give you all you could ever want." He gestured with the hammer below the windshield. After a few minutes of staring, the thin man got back in his car and sat. Ralph blinked his lights again. The faggot stuck his head out the window and Ralph waved the hammer at him. The man's engine started, and he began to pull away. Ralph leaped out of the cab and threw the hammer. It shattered the back window, strewing splinters of glass in front of the truck. The sedan sped onto the highway with glass tinkling in its wake.

"Faggot," Ralph bellowed. "You fucking faggot. No truckers tonight." He laughed and got back in the cab.

CHAPTER 23

Children

I am on my way to trial, where the government attorney will call a lady from the draft board as his first witness. She is big and has her hair tied on top of her head. She will testify as to who I am and what I was ordered to do. Then the attorney will call an army lieutenant and an FBI agent to testify as to what I didn't do. It will all take thirty minutes. The lieutenant and the FBI agent will leave as soon as they testify. They are busy men.

The highway funnels into Morgan Hill for a series of stoplights. Traffic is backed up for three blocks. The drugstore across the street is advertising new faces for a dollar a tube. In the side street behind it, there are screams coming from the elementary school playground.

The children are taken early. They collect into a young river, trickling from the arterial side streets and courtyards, and approach the school in a torrent of lunch pails and hair ribbons. Some are ferried in cars. The front steps of the school swarm with little bodies scurrying out of automobiles

116

and through the front doors. The schoolside corners are manned by the safety patrol in white canvas Sam Browne belts and yellow flannel hats that look like inverted envelopes. Most of the patrol is sternly occupied with their responsibility, and those who aren't are jealous of the bicycle riders doing tricks near the playground fence. You can hear the bell ring for two blocks around the school. At the moment of its piercing sound, the playground begins to empty, and in five minutes only the misfits are not yet tucked into a room. When they finally arrive they are given tardy notices and made to stay after school. After such acts of discipline, including the salute of the flag, comes spelling and then arithmetic, followed by the first recess.

The first recess lasts only ten minutes. It is too short for organized play and can only be an explosion. The boy they call Tom the Spider is doing cartwheels in front of a crowd. Everyone is screaming—not at anything in particular, but simply because they have held all their screams through the flag salute and spelling and arithmetic and must now scream them all so that they can remain quiet until lunch. Two boys from the third row of Mrs. Jenkin's class are snickering at little Sally who never wears underwear and insists on playing hopscotch. She doesn't seem to notice and thinks only of her pet frog. Once again the bell, and the square block of sound empties into the silent red brick of the buildings. Until lunch, there will be history.

Before the recess is forgotten, Mrs. Whooper has sent Sally to the principal. The principal, Mr. Cagletti, who has a heavy face with smudges of black whiskers, sends her home to put on some underwear. After she left for the principal's office, Mrs. Whooper went through Sally's desk and found a dead field mouse and three marbles hidden under her speller. In the sixth-grade class, Darlene, who will be married before the eighth grade, is writing notes to another Sally about how she is in love with Donald, who sleeps in the back row. The fourth graders are reading about the Yakutat Indians and watching the clock in the middle of the wall. Rushing to noon, lunch seems to stumble just before it is about to happen and takes an infinity to again reach its feet and open the doors of the brick rooms. In school, one learns that clocks are slow.

Everyone is required to eat before they play. The playground equipment is not made available until twelve thirty. The teachers march their classes out of the rooms in long double-file lines into the cafeteria, with the double files spreading to triple, quadruple, and no file at all when out of the teachers' gaze. In the lunchroom they are broken into two groups—those who have brought their lunches in sacks and pails and those who have tokens to buy hot lunches. The tokens are brass coins with square holes in the middle. The line to the hot-lunch counter is full of children on their knees looking for the coins they just dropped.

The lunches all look familiar. The plates are plastic with indentations that divide the brown surface into three sections. In the upper right-hand corner there are always peas or beets. If there are peas, they are soggy. If there are beets, they are scarlet and couched in a runny syrup that soon laps over its dikes and infests the mashed potatoes and on to the two boiled frankfurters until all of the lunch swims in a dilute plasma solution. Irving Hordung eats everything on his plate, including the peas or beets. Tom the Spider drops the peas one by one onto the floor until his plate's pea pocket is empty, and he is excused onto the playground before anyone sees the floor. In school, one learns to deal with peas.

Outside, the noisy horde breaks into gangs, and the gangs are organized into teams that play against each other. The bigger kids play softball, while the smaller ones kick rubber balls and throw them at each other. The fourth graders march around the playground pretending they are an army. Mr. Bolt, the fourth-grade teacher in Room 14, is leading them. His lieutenant is Samuel Miller, who runs up and down the line, shouting left and right and shuffling his feet.

On the softball field, which is solid asphalt like the rest of the playground, Tom the Spider has just slid on his stomach half the distance between second and third base. The knees of his jeans are completely gone and his hands have turned to a bloody pulp. But he is safe, and he beams as Mrs.

119

Jenkins takes him to the nurse. The game loses its flash after Tom the Spider leaves, so the bigger kids break up the game and retire to raiding the jungle gym where they scare the wits out of the first graders. These playground initiates are saved by the bell and are happy to go back in the building. When one is young, one learns that there is safety in age.

The afternoon is slow. The sweat from the softball game doesn't dry until geography is finished. Before English there is show and tell. Alice Glick has brought all of her father's medals from the war, and Jaimie Waller a rock with six colors and four peacock feathers. Tom the Spider is sent to the principal for pulling off his bandages and putting them on Karen Molokoff's desk. She screams, he laughs, and Mrs. Jenkins opens the door.

The last recess is only ten minutes and is simply a teaser for the end of school. Little Sally, back wearing underwear, is playing hotscotch. To go with her underwear, she brought her pet frog.

After English class, the last bell sounds. The school explodes with children darting everywhere; they coagulate for a few minutes in the playground and then break into little groups picking their way along the gutters toward home. The safety patrol is out, envying the bicycle riders, and the Banducci brothers chase James Peters all the way to Federal Avenue, where he escapes into the gas station and through the blind man's yard in back of it.

The judge will spend an hour and a half instrucing the jury as to their duties to uphold and enforce the law. He will say it ponderously and over again four times.

"Your duty is not to rule on the law itself. You must apply the law. That is your sworn duty as members of the jury. What you think of the law doesn't matter in this court. That is a decision for other people to make. Congress must decide those questions. The question you must decide is whether or not the defendant did on January 17 of this year refuse to report for induction into the United States Army. That is the only question you have to answer."

Then the jury will go into the jury room, which also has no windows.

Leaving Morgan Hill behind. The pace picks up and the cars are moving along at sixty miles an hour through a short open stretch and then past lines of fruit stands and over the creek, where a side road leads off to the missile plant.

CHAPTER 24

Toward Trial

Now the highway is encased in itself. It dips below the level of the ground, and its sides rise at concrete angles. Then it rises on pillars, and the panorama of the passing cities stretches below it, marked and hidden by signs giving green and white directions. A row of antennas appears on the right and leads into the big air force base. The planes swoop in over the highway and land beyond its edge. They taxi to the huge hangers where twelve of their fellows are sitting with dismantled engines swarmed over by small figures. Most of the planes have circled red crosses on their sides. They fly in regularly, laden with wounded for the hospital that stands twenty-four stories on the other side of the road. Big hospital buses meet them and ferry their cargo under the rising freeway to the wards and plasma solutions standing over the city.

I will sit in a leather chair at the long table assigned to the defense. Francis will sit beside me, mulling over the papers from his briefcase. Then he will stand up and present our case. It will be a simple case, composed of my testimony and that of my mother. My mother, beautiful and Christian in her pink suit, will testify that she raised me to make up my own mind and that, as far as she could tell, I had. I will testify from the small wooden fort designed for that purpose. From it, I will be able to see all of the faces in the room. The third row will be full of grandmothers who come to all of the Resistance trials. Next to the grandmothers, there will be a guy named Joe. Joe is fat. He will come to me in the hall and say, "If I could cross my fingers, I would cross them for you." Joe's fingers are so fat, the best he will be able to do is lean one against the other. He will hold them up to me anyway. I will testify that what I did is the only thing I could imagine doing. I will say that I can't imagine us surviving any other way. "People can't live and kill each other both," I will say. The judge will note that in his book and warn Francis against asking me leading questions.

I can see San Francisco now. It begins with a long line of buildings edge to edge ascending the side of a slope in uniform pinks and yellows. They top the slope and then move down its other side until they reach the bay. The closer they get to the water's edge, the houses lose their color and figures begin to lean against their sides. From the bay, the city moves along the water's edge in shops and warehouses that swing west and stop south of Market Street. From the air, they must look like a big comma. At the top of the comma, the Federal Building stands twenty stories with fountains in front. I will be tried there. Twelve blocks below it, Market Street is cluttered with pawnshops, greasy cafes, and movie houses. Below it is Mission Street. Mission is the same, except there aren't any movie houses.

CHAPTER 25

Old Men
and Losers

By the time the morning haze has been sent running, breaking fast retreat before the sun, the men have found their places. The old men, with canes and myopia, find their way to the tables in the middle of the park. The tables were once painted in the calm logic of black and white squares with wooden lockers stapled to their ends to hold the sets of checkers and chess. The playing area is faded and scratched now. The last table on the end has a gouge running the length of the checkerboard. It was left there by an old Greek at the end of his third straight loss to a checker-wielding cripple. The old men must wait until close to noon to begin playing. The tables are still heavy with dew, and they will not dry until the sun is high enough to find its way through the overhanging trees.

The park is a square in the middle of the city. The streets edging the park are lined with bars, pool halls, and a few crumbling cinema palaces. An

optometrist on the second floor of a pool hall announces his presence with a pair of neon spectacles
and a large blinking "CREDIT." The younger men
lounge on the sidewalks. They lean on the walls
and telephone poles. They wait. They are too
young to toddle into death behind checkerboards,
so they wait for something better. They have no
work, and there is no work in sight, but they have
been waiting long enough to know that the work
they may be offered is waiting also. It is just waiting in better circumstances. They help each other
wait. When one waits with a bottle of wine
wrapped in a paper sack, three or four wait with
him. One man's tobacco or pack of cigarettes is
activity for a whole corner. The gutters are brown
with the tobacco juice of waiting. These gutters
stand as a mute offering to a deity of patience that
is by force of circumstances the patron saint of
these men. At noon the bars open, and with a glass
of beer these men can watch television for a few
hours until they are forced to buy another beer or
leave. The men all know each other, not by name
but by condition.

The train tracks are three blocks from the back-
side of the square. A constant group clusters
around the tracks. They have given up trying to
get out of waiting and try simply to get away from
it. Their leader is an Indian called Low Foot. His
left leg stops abruptly at the knee. When he finally
returned to the mainland at the end of the war, he
got a medal for what once connected his leg to the

ground. The grocery opens at eight, and one of Low Foot's band toddles back and forth from the park for the rest of the day. The men sit under the abandoned water tower, and if they are lucky they will be allowed to reach unconsciousness there. If they aren't, they will be rousted out by the railroad bull who patrols in the afternoon. When they can't sit under the water tower, they stagger to a corner of the park where they are often found retching in the flower beds. Only half of them are able to hide themselves well enough in the park. The others are taken by the police patrol and dry themselves out in a work camp for the next thirty days.

Late in the afternoon the whorehouses open. This is of little use to the senile old men or poor young men, but it brings new faces around the park. There is an influx of soldiers and sailors and men with clean shirts. The young men, who have been waiting all day, push against the walls and abandon the corners to the hookers. They work out of the old hotels, and the less established work out of the park itself. With the approach of dark, business gets heavier as the bars are crowded with sweaty men trying to forget about work until the next morning. By now the old men have gone to their separate places to sleep until the next day's checkers. Some of the young men stand in the alleys and listen for the approach of drunk soldiers.

The movies open at six. The marquee of the old theater announces that in addition to the regularly featured Humphrey Bogart movies, there is bingo at eight. In the dark theater, men sleep in the seats close to the walls. As Bogart reaches for the woman's lips, there is a shriek and a scuffle in the front rows. A truck driver is thrashing a drunk. The drunk stumbles up the isle while the truck driver hits him. While the trucker and his girl friend were watching the movie, the drunk stood up, faced them, and hung his penis over the seat. The drunk is dragged from the theater by the bouncers. "Filthy. You filthy pig." A washerwoman, who plays bingo before work, is standing and shouting. She turns to the audience and explains, "That man hit him first, but he did something nasty." No one in the audience seems to have really noticed.

After the plot is resolved with Bogart's death, bingo begins. Everyone is given a card as they enter the theater. The manager strides to the stage and calls numbers. Next to him is a board with twenty stars hanging on it. When the stars are lifted, an amount of money is revealed. The amounts range from one to twenty dollars. As the numbers progress, people call out "bingo" from the dingy seats and go up on the stage to pick a star. After twenty minutes, only three stars are left. The top prize of twenty dollars has yet to be taken. The next number is "42," and three more people file up onto the stage. The first is an old black man in working clothes. He chooses the orange star with green speckles and wins a dollar. The second is a clerk at an all-night drugstore who picks the blue star and wins twenty dollars. He will buy one of the big boxes of candy when he leaves work the next morning and give it to his girl friend, the hairdresser. The last star is white and brown, and the drunk sailor who is left by default wins five dollars. He and his buddies cheer as he walks up the aisle to his seat. Most of the crowd will leave before the next movie and wait for the following Wednesday, when their luck may be better.

CHAPTER 26

Cages

It is the next day. I have walked to a point above the neck of the bay where I can watch the shipping pass into the harbor. The ships come in with their big whistles and a trail of chop washes against the rock face of the city where it drops down to a thin beach. The ships pass behind the island prison of Alcatraz. Alcatraz is empty, with cobwebs growing on the cell doors and rust collecting on the barbed wire. The morning paper carries a story about a prison rebellion in Ohio. The rebellion was quelled by an army of police and national guard.

There are very few of them left now. They sealed the cellblock off four days ago. There were close to a hundred then. They all had done it without plan, but with the energy that had been piling in their veins for all the years they had been prisoners. It was not something they had known with the front of their lives; it was not a sudden blindness; it was the balance of years, years spent in cages and under orders. In prison, it is the random drip day after day that inundates the fields.

The talk of it had begun the day Kitchen Shorty got out of isolation. He had just finished seven days in a five-by-five cell with a hole in the floor and a mattress the guard threw in just before lights out. He had been pulled from his job in the cook shack for back talk to the guard. It was the tall skinny guard with the hooked nose. Shorty told him to fuck off, and in fifteen minutes his solitary time began. When they brought him back to the cellblock, Shorty didn't talk for the whole night. He had been beaten twice, once very badly. He seemed to nurse himself, licking his wounds and glaring between the strips of parallel iron. The first thing he said was said between tightly gripped lips. "No more," he said, and the words had a cutting edge that made everyone at the mess table turn and look, not with question but with shock. Shorty hit them with cold water. It was time.

The guards knew something was happening during the next week. No one had told, it was just that the concrete houses of the Ohio State Penitentiary offer no nooks and crannies into which one might stuff the manifestations of thought. It is a one dimensional world with every man trapped in a single plane. The guards could feel the energy of the cellblock. They felt it walking the tiers of cell fronts, and they felt it as they watched the tiny figures in the yard from watch towers. Something was coming. Like the steady compression of heat before storms, the men were brewing. In their minds, they were preparing to thread the eye of the needle, to leap through the tiny hole in time into a new set of days. They had no idea what they might get. Shorty had said it for all of them: "No more."

When it happened, it felt like a relief. Shorty and Sampson and two of the lifers grabbed the guards, while Jones and Korpultsky grabbed the guns from the guard room. Five more guards came in and were quickly disarmed. Then the rebels sealed the building with the gate controls. The hundred prisoners now had their own fort. It was stocked with bits and pieces of food that they had smuggled and hid in the last week and four shotguns, eleven revolvers, and an automatic rifle. For the first hour, they all shouted and banged cups on the walls and bars. For this moment they were, in the only sense they could understand, free.

The guards tried to retake the building once. They were repulsed by the steady if erratic fire of the prisoners' weapons. One guard was wounded and dragged out of reach of the bullets, leaving a bloody trail in the yard. The guards tried tear gas, but the canisters never made it into the cellblock and fizzled harmlessly against one of the walls. The night was quiet, and the prisoners took turns guarding their stronghold. The next morning, the prison authorities had drawn battle lines across the yard. There were barricades, and behind the barricades were guards and state troopers.

Walking behind them all was the warden, a fat man in shirt sleeves. He was wearing dark glasses and talking stiffly to his army. His jaws, beneath the roll of cheek that extended along their length, gripped a cigar stub and betrayed the mounting energy of his anger. He would have no peace until the cellblock was back to proper order. He picked up a megaphone and told the men arranged at the windows of the mighty steel cage that if they surrendered now, there would be no reprisals.

The men inside looked at each other with a grim laugh. Shorty shouted back, "Not till you agree with our grievances. No more rousting for cigarettes and shit from the guards."

"No more beatings, Korpultsky screamed.

"Give us more time in the yard," a lifer shouted.

Suddenly all the barred windows were full of faces shouting until the yard was a cacophony of wailing complaint. The warden turned and disappeared into his office. The rest of the second day was quiet.

During the night they heard activity outside the walls. In the morning there was a national guard troop behind the barricades. Standing next to the short-sleeved warden was a tall man in uniform. He wore an iron helmet that came down over his ears. The guardsmen had assault rifles and fired regularly into the building. Mickey, the annoying pickpocket doing six to twelve, got a bullet in the forehead. Shorty ran to the window with one of the captured guards. He held the guard up to the

light and fired his pistol point-blank into his brain.
The firing stopped.

The first tear gas hit in the afternoon of the third
day. It boiled up through the tiers of cells, and men
ran choking and scratching their eyes and throats.
When the gas finally cleared, fifty-seven men had
run into the yard and were in the hands of the men
behind the barricades. Before the evening fell
black and hard on the state prison outside of
Akron, all but the remaining fourteen had left in
the midst of a second tear gas attack.

It is now the fourth day. Shorty's eyes are red,
and the veins in his hands stand out like small
ropes running up his forearms and under his shirt.
He has not slept in all of the four days. The body
of the dead prisoner is in an empty cell. It has begun to smell. On the bunk facing it is the body of
the guard. Both sets of vacant eyes are trained on
the ceiling. Eight captured guards are kept in a
huddle by Jones and his rifle. The megaphone outside is still shouting "surrender." Shorty fires his
pistol out the window in disgust. They look at each
other and know they must surrender. The door to
the cellblock is swung open, and the captured
guards are shoved out.

"We're surrendering," Shorty shouts. The guards
run to the shelter of the barricades. Shorty shouts
again, "We're surrendering." There is no answer
from behind the barricades. Korpultsky starts out
the door and is hit in the leg with a bullet. "We're
surrendering, I said." Shorty can hardly shout now.

His throat is raw. There has been no water for the last day. The soldiers look over their shoulders to the warden. He stands with his arms folded across his belly. His eyes are hidden behind dark glasses. He will not hear what Shorty is saying. Shorty screams his armistice for a final time, and the men look to the warden. He looks straight ahead without movement. After two minutes, he signals, and the firing begins again. The men in the cellblock only look at each other. Shorty is loading his pistol and muttering "son of a bitch" to himself. Two of the men try to surrender and are cut down in the middle of the yard. In half an hour there is no prison rebellion outside of Akron. Fourteen bodies are hoisted into the back of a truck and driven through the gates of the State Prison and down the thin line of concrete that runs up to the walls like the stem of some giant plant.

The judge will sentence me at nine thirty in the evening. The building will be empty except for the courtroom where he sits. "Normally," he will say, "sentence is a question of rehabilitation. You can't be rehabilitated, and you don't want to be rehabilitated."

"But," he will continue, looking over the top of his glasses, "you will be punished. I sentence you to serve three years in a federal prison to be chosen by the Justice Department." Then he will dismiss the court. The long white tubes of light will flicker off, and he will close his leatherbound book.

Alcatraz is still there. With binoculars you can

see the guard posts and behind them the yard covered with shadow. Tomorrow I will go on trial. When it's over I will be in one of Alcatraz's younger brothers. I don't feel like I'm leaving America so much as just getting in a little deeper.

CHAPTER 27

The Great
Comic Bird

I will always think of my trial as the trial of the great comic bird. The judge sits behind his glasses at the elevated rostrum, and over his head a mosaic seal of the United States is nailed to the wall. The eagle on the seal has an anvil-shaped head. Its top is long and flat, and where one might find a face, an enormous beak grows out of the skull and runs from the crest of the head to the bottom of the throat. Juror number seven, a Filipino with a balding round skull that bulges out from under the remnants of his hair, will spend the entire trial staring at that bird. Occasionally, while the judge is rambling through a long monologue, I look up and think I am being tried by Walt Disney.

The judge is a short man named Carter. He wears enormous, brightly colored bow ties and parts his hair in the middle. He has risen from the state legislature to his position as federal judge. His father held the same judgeship before him and he, like his father, is proud of his experience on the bench and his self-made concern with the process of order and social defense he knows as the law. He comes to the courtroom each day from his chambers, a large office lined with identically bound volumes where the monotony of law library is broken only by a desk and table piled with paper and files. A photographic portrait of his wife and daughter balance the desk.

When I go to his chambers to listen to him and the lawyers discussing legal points, he sits back in his chair and moves only his glasses for the sake of an occasional eye rub. His eyes are half closed most of the time, and in a moment of strain, when called upon to exercise his control, they blink rapidly. His speech is slow, each word sounding as though it has been extracted from his throat. The spoken word is a meticulous and careful operation for him. Nevertheless, when he speaks, he speaks at great length if not with volume, with occasional flourishes back through previously mentioned points in the hopes of further exacting and qualifying that which will never assume the flat and even surface he desires. He relates to his words like a sheep dog to a grazing flock of sheep, urging them slowly onward and yapping around the perimeters to keep them in a solid mass. He thinks of himself as a referee, the overseer of movements between conflicting parties. His interest is in the law itself, whose endless volumes seem to rest on his back like a great weight or a flying buttress.

Without statutes, men have only themselves, and to Judge Carter having oneself is synonymous with doom and chaos. He has come to judge as the high priest of order, of conflict and progress—the arbiter between man and the society by which man is ruled. Judge Carter has come to direct and maintain a civilization under constant threat from the existence of the men who form its substance.

The various officials of the court are seated in front of the judge's dais: the crier, the recorder, the clerk, and the judge's legal aide. The clerk and the recorder sit on a plateau directly below that of the judge. The crier sits in a command post by the jury box and rises to announce the judge's comings and goings and keep the people from standing in the aisles. All three of these men—the recorder, the clerk, and the crier—are friendly in the course of their business, dressed neatly in cheap suits and are without mouths. Theirs is the role of perpetual silence, and their faces are distinguished by lines where one looks for lips. The fourth is a thin young man with a soft face. He hangs on to the edges of the judge in an office chair below the clerk. They, the valets of the judge's justice, never seem to notice the trial save as it creates tasks.

These men administer justice. Justice to them is a process of maintaining the law in an established equation of hearing and dispute. The disputing parties are myself and the government of the United States. The government maintains that I have violated the Selective Service Act. <u>I maintain that America has violated life itself.</u>

Justice is a word with a Latin root that translates literally as "that which is fitting." In the abstract, justice is a matter of proportions. Doing justice is fashioning a proper relationship between things, the integration of a form. It gains its meaning from what is considered proper. The propriety that defines justice was decided long before I ever got near the long dark wooden table sitting below the gaze of the judge. Justice is being administered by the state, which must reconcile the world to itself. The formalities of this justice are to be carried out by a jury. The jury is to do justice to the judge, the judge to the law, the law to the state, and the state to itself.

The first juror, a divorcee with short black hair, is from Alameda. Her neighborhood swarms with the explosions of jets breaking from the bonds of sound as they rise out of the naval air station. The second is a polite young black man whose family all live in Arkansas. The third is a young blond accountant who does income tax for the rich who live along the skyline in Burlingame. The fourth is a balding man whose face drops immediately past his lips and leaves the appearance of being without a chin. His head is constantly tucked under, and his hand is wrapped about the bottom of his face in an effort to hide the swift grade from his lip to his neck. The fifth is a Quaker woman with a son in the army. The sixth is an executive trainee from the Shell Oil Company. The gates of the Shell Oil plant are flanked with union pickets each morning. The seventh is the balding Filipino who was made a citizen after he learned to say the flag salute aloud in English. The eighth is a small black woman who works as a domestic on Jackson Street. The judge's language seems to pass over her tiny stature, leaving her oblivious to the legal proceedings. The ninth is a very big white woman with her hair piled into a beehive on the top of her head. She sits with her head slanted back and looks along the line of her nose toward the judge. The tenth is a black housewife who does volunteer work with the Salvation Army. The last two are elderly women. One stares constantly at the judge. The other stares at her feet. As they are officially seated, they all swear that they hold no preconceived judgments.

After two days of testimony and eight hours of deliberation, the jury has determined my guilt. The judge has pronounced my sentence. With the authority and wisdom handed down from the great comic bird, my life has been ladled into a row of cells stretching along a corridor lit with blue lights.

The space in my cell is tangible. There is nowhere it might spread to make room for my presence, so it is compressed here with me and the reflections of the blue light. The light is caught on Arthur's skin as he sleeps in the opposite bunk. In this light I can see my wife walking around with her belly protruding from the weight of a new life.

I can see the judge rubbing his eyes in deliberation. I can see the dead marching into the sea as a final sanctification of their condition.

The muffled sounds of Crazy Leon sneak into the corridor under the iron door. He screams every night because his cell is full of faces. Mine is too.

CHAPTER 28

Life and Death

We know where we are. We are in America. Where we are going is the remaining question. It is a question of life and death.

When I say life and death, I mean more than the physical states in which the body either functions or does not. These two states are the visible expression and obvious consequence of larger directions. The ancient Greeks understood life and death as *Eros* and *Thanatos,* two conflicting universal forces with which existence is shaped.

Eros, the life force, drives men to extend themselves, to build, to create larger and larger constructions. It is the force that impels men beyond themselves in search of a more inclusive being. It is growth and fruition, birth and revelation, transcendence and expression. It is the gathering of a common whole—that which seeks to encompass all and everything through all and everything. It bridges the separate and joins the scattered. It seeks to extend each of us to a point where we join and touch those around us. It is in the artist's brush, the craftsman's hammer, the farmer's hoe, and the mother's breast. It accomplishes the universal through the extension and enlargement of each. *Eros* is affirmation, a common and inclusive reality. It is everything.

Thanatos, the force of death, accomplishes the universal through the diminution of each. It is the negation. In following this force, man follows his own nonexistence, and we wither and decay. *Thanatos* is the barren, that from which nothing grows. It breaks the world into a multiplicity of separate existences and then atrophies each in his isolation. Instead of bringing together, it breaks apart. It is antithesis and repulsion as opposed to synthesis and attraction. It pursues conflagration and annihilation. It narrows and divides, shatters and disperses. It has unity only in negation, the unity found in an omniscient nothing. As we pursue death, we diminish ourselves with separate and exclusive realities. The dead cannot see; for them, there is no reality beyond each of their particulars. Whereas *Eros* urges us to grow, *Thanatos* drives us to cease.

Each of these is a direction man might pursue. We pursue them in our doing. Doing America is a direction as well as a location. Since each of us experiences, each of us is a source of knowledge about man. I am unable to speak for us all. I will speak for myself. The America I have experienced, for all of its potential comfort, is death to man. America, like man, is a process with inherent char-

144

acteristics. The foremost of those characteristics is that whatever the policy, the basis of its existence is our continual diminution. In it, our lives cease to exist. We have been superseded by the life of the state: when we might bloom, we are directed; when we might learn, we are instructed; when we might heal, we are wounded; when we might see, we are told to mask ourselves and pretend that what is, isn't, and that what isn't, never will be.

As it goes on, the American state pursues the necessities and expressions implicit in its existence. History lists those necessities and expressions as the manufacture and unleashing of poisons on man, beast, and plant alike, the gathering of the most immense stock of destruction in man's known existence, the organization of itself into poor and rich, exploiters and exploited, those who buy and sell each other. Ingrained in the face of its order, the American necessity is one of oppression and butchery, starvation and corpulence, blindness and division, stultification and misery— a bloody, agonizing, sometimes comfortable pursuit of noth-ingness. These necessities are synonymous with death brought to form in social organization. As it pursues its existence, the American state logically concludes in our absence from the face of the earth. I look around, and we seem to be calm and satiated in the illusions of a path leading to the edge of the abyss. Each step along the way kills.

The only response to America I can imagine is life itself.

CHAPTER 29

The Revolution

The manisfestation of life is a politics. It means engendering and sustaining a reality.

Building a reality is work. It is a construction. Such work is neither simple to do nor without the necessity of struggle, effort, and price. The point is that it must be done. I see the doing of it in three overlapping efforts.

The point of the work is people. The work is done, and in the doing of it, people's lives are shaped. The progression of any politics is the formation of those within it. The shaping and growth of those lives is also the work. The politics of life is a way of doing. The heart of it is a new man. Taking our particular lives as a beginning, this means that a repetition of the patterns and forms of America, a repetition of the doing of the state, is a redressing and not a new politics. The basis of the work is in the lives of those who do it. Those lives are its seeds. Out of them grows whatever is to follow. The work exists ontologically, as a process of being. The first expression of a new politics

146

is in its notion of means. It is a new *how* of living and, therefore, *new living* beings.

At present, the lives America encloses are its property—the extension of America in deed if not always in words. Exercising a new *how* of living is the reclaiming of those lives. Lives are reclaimed in developing and acting out their own terms. What the state has usurped is repossessed. The *how* of life's politics is a function of each of us. The hope of the work is that an indigenous reality will grow from it, which means that this new politics is lived as a right of those who live it. As a whole, the politics declares that each person's life is his own. The initial expression of that is lives exercised as the people who possess them see fit. The politics takes root in an individual consciousness. It is then practiced in all the small and large patterns of people's living. It comes forward as a behavior. It begins by taking our lives as our own to be exercised accordingly. Given our condition, this an act of defiance to the state.

Such repossession (and implicit defiance) is not in itself a politics or an alternative reality. Without further extension, it seems to be a dead end which may produce monmentary enjoyment but not qualitative change. The development of a new reality hinges on the way it is done. The way it is done is the birth of a new process. It is the extension of that new process which takes form as a politics. A new politics is an operative set of values.

Honesty and openness are implicit in a politics of life, which reclaims lives with these forces. The object is to bring about a synthesis of lives into a common whole, and inclusive reality. This is only possible if those lives are available. Within the functioning of the state, lives are permeated with hidings and secrecies, with boundaries and strict division into public and private existences. This simply means that we never know or reveal who or what we are to each other. We don't ever experience others wholly; we experience them as a function of the state. Commonality is impossible in that situation. Commonality will be reached only by bringing people out of hiding, not placing them in it. The open act of reclamation of lives as a politics is not the claim to a separate and private life; it is the furthering of a reality permeated with an indigenous existence. It is an initial embodiment. It is an act of sharing, not isolation—of stepping out, not stepping in. This means that the act of reclamation is a beginning of a politics. Its beginning and its continuation must be available in order to exist. They are open by definition.

The politics of life is done with any number of motivations. There are two that strike me as of utmost importance. The first is that we do it because our lives depend on it. I find it impossible to live without a new politics. The exercise of a life that is real to the person living it is impossible in the confines of the state. We do it because we don't exist without it. Its reality is our own. The

148

second is that it is done because we care not just for ourselves or our notion of politics but about all of those lives around us. Reclaiming one's life is a step toward a whole reality, and as such is an act of compassion. We are attempting to bring benefit to our brothers. This compassion is an expression of a fundamental in the politics of life: the idea that all men's lives are sacred. If that is our politics, then compassion must supplant anger and caring supplant righteousness.

As a strategy, the practice of this politics works in its own pattern. Let us look at how people learn. It is most obvious in young children, but it is true of us all. We learn not by what others say but what they do. (We are all watched by each other. We watch and are watched in an attempt to understand what we might do. Because of that, we all have a constituency, some small, some large.) It is not the statement but the practice of a reality that makes it available. If we seek a reality with our politics, then it is possible only if that reality is practiced as well as spoken of. It is the deed and not the word that man is contained in. If we are talking of a reality in which men are as they choose to be—a reality that grows from its constituent lives—then our relation to men must reflect that to give it any possibility. If it is a world in which people are cared for, we must care; if men are to be free, we must attempt to demonstrate the behavior of free men. Our doing of life is all that makes it possible for anyone else.

149

If we don't do life, it ceases to exist. A reality grows through participation. It is acted out. The reality we seed must be done and open to others' doing. A politics of life will grow because it is experienced.

If this politics grows as it is experienced, then we must work to make it grow by being it. We will not be it completely, for we are not its completion. We are its beginning. But we can seek the closest possible approximation. We pass it on and extend it in what we do. This being the case, it is obviously a politics that makes no separation between means and ends. The politics is itself first. It is a notion of man that is carried in its process. It is new life. It doesn't define itself by its negation. A politics defined by its negation is never free of that negation. If the negation were to cease, so would the politics.

Life exists as an *is*, not an *is not*. It negates, but as a function of its own growth, like a seed breaking the earth with its sprout. As it realizes itself, it breaks through the state. But it does so as an affirmation. Its affirmation is carried in the everyday reality of the politics. It does and in doing, grows. It is more than a path leading to an object. The politics is the totality of the journey. Its values and processes are no postponements to a point in future time. They are now. If they aren't, they aren't real. If A, then A; if B, then B. It practices a phenomenal logic: what is, is. If the politics of life is, it will reflect itself and not its adversaries. It will make its own terms and not accept those of the existing state.

Both the old and the new are what they do. In making life, we must do our future in our present. This process begins with establishing our existence in the face of the state—doing our terms.

If the first effort seems to center on the individual, the second is the birth of the collective. Community is a realization of the politics of life. The growth of the politics creates a set of processes and a mutual existence of those engaged. Community is the exercise of that mutual existence.

A community is organized; it is arranged. As it grows, it becomes an alternative to the state. Its processes make it an alternative. As the politics grow, we gather together, we arrange the gathering. The work is to find an arrangement that reflects the life we wish to extend.

I think the key to that arrangement is the idea of fraternity. There are two possible locations of authority within a gathering—paternal and fraternal. The paternal expresses a reality that is done over people. It is the function of the father ruling the family. Its organization is a very standard pyramid structure. Reality is passed down to dependents. The fraternal is not a layered structure of one over the other. It is a posturing that exists on a single plane. We are next to each other. Its arrangement presumes the equal value of all those it includes. It is not father to son, but brothers and sisters to brothers and sisters. Its existence is not a function of one or a few, but a function of the collective itself.

A community's reality is everyone in it. The authority exercised in that reality rests in the dynamic that makes the community a single entity. Its authority is a function of the process of coming together. It is the authority and order of harmony. Its arrangement must reflect that harmony. Fraternal authority rests in the mutual process of cohesion. That mutual cohesion is the source of its reality.

Fraternity is a process of sharing. Sharing is the community's availability to itself. If we exist together, our resources are common. The community is co-operated. Sharing permeates all of its form. The sharing of decisions is not a question of the larger group enforcing itself on the smaller, or vice versa. Sharing decisions is approaching them as a common body. In the process of decision making, this common body must be retained. The model for this arrangement is not voting, but consensus. A decision is made when it can commonly be accepted and engaged in. The community makes decisions together and not apart.

The community creates a range of processes which exist as the fiber of the work. It is the skeletal structure. As the state is broken through, the community takes over its functions. The community is the concretization of the politics, not in its final substance, for it continues to include in

152

larger circles, but in its full, if germinal, form. It too exists now and not soon.

The community exists not only in relation to itself but to the rest of the world. Its relation to that world is threefold: (1) It holds the symbolic position as an embodiment of the politics. It is the demonstrative working model. The way the work is organized is what remains when the state crumbles. Its existence teaches and realizes the politics. The community is experienced by whatever surrounds it. (2) The collective is a source of energy for its participants and their work. It is a base from which we engage ourselves in the construction of larger realities. It is the source of sustenance and education internally. Its context provides a setting for the development of new identities and visions. In it, we teach each other. The community is an avenue for further understanding. It houses an ongoing discovery. The community is experienced by those within it. (3) The community is inclusive. It grows. It is the area of expression for those drawn into the work. As they seek to make it real, the community expands as their realization. The community may have any number of physical existences in any number of places, but it is held together as a common embodiment of the process of a politics. As the edges of the politics extend, the community includes. It is the new reality in progress.

As the politics grows, it enters larger and larger encounters with the state. Its growth is in conflict.

Conflict is a function of political growth. I think that is an important distinction. It means that the conflict is not within an existing reality but between two realities. The stakes are the existence of one or the other. One will extend and the other recede. We understand this conflict as practiced by the state by the word "repression." The state attempts to eliminate other realities. It does this by establishing the priority of its terms among the people. It diminishes other realities by imposing itself.

Successful repression seems to have two stages: first, the alternative reality is emasculated. Force is exercised to alter it into something consumable by the state, and then it is consumed. The state represses by making its opponents into its reflection and then its substance. The state uses its available force to direct the conflict according to its priorities. The conflict then takes place on its ground. This is its first success in diminishing the others' reality. It will stage the conflict between two states within the acceptance of the state's political processes. At that point, the outcome is a question of one interest superseding the other, not a conflict between politics. If the state is successful, the new reality becomes an old process with a fresh face.

In this conflict, a new politics must both maintain itself and grow. The question involved is one of power. Not simply over the possession of power but over the nature of power itself. A new politics

154

entails a new power in both substance and form. If it adopts the state's power in order to wage a struggle, it ceases to be a new politics. The real struggle is not to seize power, but to transform it. The new politics grows, it doesn't conquer. When it loses its existence as a reality distinguishable from that of the state, it has lost itself.

I think a politics of life will encounter the state at three primary points: the use of force (where the state practices militarism and imperialism), the arrangement of resources (where the state is based upon capitalism and nationalism), and the locus of power (where the state is paternal, authoritarian, and inherently totalitarian).

A politics based on the idea of life itself comes forward very clearly. It is a participatory process, in which the participants have an immediate and indigenous relation to reality. In that process, men govern themselves in common association based on consensus. It is an arrangement of resources according to need. It seeks the common benefit of all. It does not recognize property, either within itself or as a function of its total existence.

This politics does not establish itself as a property in a word broken into separate properties. Both capitalism and nationalism are anathema to it. Because it is both participatory and shared, it is not a politics that imposes itself. It exists because people want it. It exercises a force of growth, not of destruction. It has power that the state can never have. Its power is not an ability to level its enemies, it is in bringing a realization. It engenders life, it does not steal it. It does not exist by any means. It exists as a specific means, which when violated is the end of the politics.

In the conflict with the state, we have a number of tools. The conflict takes place around the resource of authority. Both the state and the new politics need to be participated in if they are to exist, but they can't be participated in at the same time. Thus the choice of participation is a choice of realities. As the people deny the state's authority for the sake of new reality, the state loses power. A new reality can deny the state the lives it feeds off. This process continues until the orders of the state are ignored, and it splits apart like the shell of an egg, exposing a new reality. At the edges of this process, where the conflict is engaged in, it takes the form of noncooperation, occupation, boycott, strike, and organized disobedience. As these tools are used to establish a reality, the politics extends itself. America will not function without people to do it. As those lives do different, America atrophies. We engage in the conflict in an attempt to extend the experience of the politics to all involved. We organize the conflict as an experience. At each point of it, we come forward with an alternative reality to that of the police, the bankers, the functionaries, the frightened, and the lonely. Our success is that reality's concrete existence.

The politics I have attempted to describe is real

for me. It is a phenomenon of sharing, dignity, gentleness, persistence, understanding, seriousness, faith, and joy. It is a multiplicity of simultaneous processes and efforts. All together, I call them the Revolution. I don't ever see it stopping. It only grows into new dimensions.

CHAPTER 30

Love

I can offer no guarantees about the Revolution.
I don't claim to have any total understanding of
it. What I have written is a guess. As we proceed
in the Revolution, step by step, I think we will
understand much more. It is bigger than any of
us, so there will be no lack of things to learn. It
is life itself.

Eros, what the Greeks understood as the life
force, was also understood as love. I am convinced
that the Revolution will grow as we begin to understand the implications of that force. The mere
idea of it is immense. It can't be contained, only
described, like an uncharted sea. You don't push
it around, you flow with it. It brings together and
synthesizes. It makes whole the shattered and
heals the broken. It makes "we" out of what was
once "us" and "them." It denies death itself by
proclaiming and exercising our capacity for vision
and fruition. It integrates an infinite progression
of forms; it closes the circle. Its harvest lays waste
to its adversaries. It hates the sin and not the

sinner. It builds but does not beg. It calls forth the germination of man, humbles the highest, and ennobles the prostrate and used. It is the power of all men, and in it all men are strong.

If I believed the newspapers, I would know that would-be revolutionists don't talk about love. But I don't. If I believed the newspapers, I would be proud that the president gives medals to kids who have their legs shot off. I'm not. If I believed the newspapers, I would take my typewriter and sail for Tierra del Fuego. But the jailer does believe the newspapers and keeps a close eye on all of us. There doesn't seem to be anywhere to go except forward.

CHAPTER 31

I Woke This
Morning

I woke this morning to the sounds of Crazy Leon.
Down the corridor, the morning light filters
through the grated window. It casts a pink glow
that edges along the shadows toward my cell.